IN TIME OF
WAR
HAMPSHIRE

JOHN LEETE

FOREWORD BY EDMUND DE ROTHSCHILD

Sutton Publishing Limited
Phoenix Mill · Thrupp · Stroud
Gloucestershire · GL5 2BU

First published 2006

Copyright © John Leete, 2006

Title page photograph: 'Thumbs up': a
fighter pilot leaves on another mission
from a local airfield. *(Studio 54)*

British Library Cataloguing in Publication Data
A catalogue record for this book is available from the
British Library.

ISBN 0-7509-4133-2

Typeset in 10.5/13.5 Plantin.
Typesetting and origination by
Sutton Publishing Limited.
Printed and bound in England by
J.H. Haynes & Co. Ltd, Sparkford.

To 'Olly'

Dr Matt de Quincey

Collecting scrap was a vital part of the war effort on the Home Front. *(WRVS)*

Contents

Edmund de Rothschild. *(Exbury Estate)*

Foreword

It gives me the greatest pleasure to provide a foreword to John Leete's second book. John is indeed a dedicated historian and has compiled a wealth of evocative personal accounts.

I write in the year of the sixtieth anniversary of the end of the 1939–45 hostilities. In not many more years, the phrase 'in living memory' will have to be dropped from descriptions of this conflict, and it will join the countless ranks of wars consigned to history, for which no new verbal accounts can be gathered. It is for this reason that John's tapping of the diminishing, yet vivid, memories is so important. As vital is his continued attention to the experiences of those who contributed to the war effort in so many different and unrecognised ways and whose normal lives were suspended for six long years.

My contribution to the war was in a military capacity. After one difficult day of action in North Africa, the Colonel addressed my unit. He said: 'Gentlemen, you've already been through a pretty rough experience. But I want you to remember this: that things are never as bad as they seem and, conversely, they are never as good.' Life back home was defined by this kind of philosophy, as this book testifies.

Edmund de Rothschild

Wrens were based on the Exbury estate, Hampshire, home of the Rothschild family. (*Marion Loveland*)

Acknowledgements

Iam indebted to the following individuals and organisations, without whose interest this book would not have been possible. I am also grateful to all the contributors in the United Kingdom, Australia, New Zealand and the United States of America who gave me their time and support.

Special thanks go to Paul Cave, Katrina Chilton, Sharon Cross, Sally Day, Betty Driver, Michael A. Hamilton, Rowena Howes, Jackie Jones, Alastair Layzell, Alan McCormick, Mr Edmund de Rothschild, Nigel Walker, Steven Welsh; also Aldershot Military Museum, Cadbury Schweppes PLC, Colonial Pictures, John Laing PLC, New Scotland Yard, Northamptonshire Record Office, The Police Museum, Women's Royal Voluntary Service.

Always a welcome sight, the mobile tea bars played a part in keeping the spirits high. (*WVRS*)

1

Radio Days

We believe that individual liberty, rooted in human dignity, is man's greatest treasure. We believe that men, given free expression of their will, prefer freedom and self-independence to dictatorship and collectivism.

(Dwight D. Eisenhower)

The words of Dwight D. Eisenhower came to symbolise the feelings of the majority and the motivation of all who were the unwilling participants in a world war that was to change lives, attitudes, society and the future for generations to come.

In trying to understand the Second World War and how, against seemingly impossible odds, good was to triumph over evil, we need to learn from the 'ordinary' people who endured hardship to the extreme and yet remained stoic to the end. Sheer determination, the natural instinct for survival and a resolute strength were to be cornerstones of daily life in a war that harnessed the power of machinery and weapons the like of which had never been seen before.

The setbacks for this country and its allies in the early years of the war were more than compensated for after the turning point of the Battle of Britain. Although further struggles and dark days lay ahead, it is generally considered that the long slog to the eventual cessation of hostilities in both Europe and Japan began after the decisive air battles of August and September 1940.

General Eisenhower. *(US National Archives and Records Administration)*

So what of the men and women in the street, the young children who witnessed carnage and yet found adventure in spotting enemy planes, and all those personnel who went from the routine of civvy street and a close-knit community into the extraordinary world of the wartime armed services? Their stories are those of very humble folk who, having experienced the very worst of man's inhumanity to man, were able to keep body and soul together, knowing that they were fighting on the Home Front and overseas to preserve a way of life for their children and for the future of the world.

Our knowledge in the twenty-first century allows us to be more aware of what is going on about us. In the society of the 1930s and 1940s, however, few people had travelled, information about national and world affairs was not available 'at the touch of a button' and the means of communication were not as extensive and as available as they are today.

Setting the scene, Edna Hopper recalls:

We did not have a car or a telephone until long after the war. Our family remained in the town for most of the time. We lived here and worked locally. Most people only travelled out of their own little community for the annual holiday, so when the lads went off to the Army and started going out to places like Belgium, it was quite a big step for them. Suddenly they were aware of other nationalities and customs, and we had not really known about all this until the war.

Almost every family in the land had a radio, however, and it was the radio or home-made 'cat's whisker' that bought the world into the parlours and sitting

rooms of the masses. The radio did not distinguish between rich or poor, city or country dweller, politician or plumber. Maureen Sturgess fondly remembers the Ovaltineys, a radio gang show sponsored by the makers of the iconic Ovaltine brand. 'We also listened to the Rhythm Sisters, a set of quins from Scotland. I used to hear them on Radio Luxembourg and also on the BBC radio. I think they were also in a pre-war film with George Formby. Yes, that's right, it was called *Feather Your Nest*.'

The radio was an integral part of everyone's lives. (*Author's collection*)

Cadbury's chocolate, as popular then as it is today. *(Cadbury Archives)*

The radio was an integral part of life in the 1930s. It was still rather a new development, hailed as an 'exciting and magical invention to benefit everyone'. The prevailing community spirit, which was to be demonstrated beyond expectation during the coming war, was in some way endorsed by the manner in which the radio, or wireless as it was more commonly called, brought the people together. And in the years that followed, the wireless was to be used as a vital morale-boosting medium. The late Agnes Strong noted in the memoirs she prepared for her children that

Most stations only broadcast a few hours in the evening, sometimes longer during weekends. They also sent programmes from places such as nightspots outside London. This was a show called *Road House*. Apart from the cinema, the wireless was really the best and cheapest entertainment that there was for everyone. Well, everyone who could afford a wireless or who built their own, that is. It did bring most folk together, and I remember after a serious news announcement they would play a 'popular tune'. That was a way of taking our minds off what was happening, and in some way it helped as we got nearer to war. I did see one or two of the radio personalities when they appeared locally, and although they appeared well-to-do, they were very nice people – no airs and graces.

The station that, with its unique style, also remained popular with post-war generations was the previously mentioned Radio Luxembourg. This station was chosen by Cadbury in 1937 for its latest advertising venture to promote its products through a programme known as *Cadbury Calling*.

Recorded with a mix of enthusiasm, determination and a little technical know-how, the programme, which was transmitted on Saturday mornings between 8.45 and 9.15, featured stars of the day, including Reginald Dixon playing the organ at the Tower Ballroom, Blackpool. And the reason the programme went out on a Saturday was simply because a great many of the Cadbury products were bought at weekends and that was the best time to promote them. Within two years, the wireless was to become less of a promotional tool and more of a propaganda and morale-boosting machine of vital importance to the nation.

Stories, music, quiz shows and sponsors' announcements were punctuated by news bulletins. However, one piece of news that was deliberately *not* broadcast was the Government's message to local authorities on the matter of precautions in the event of air raids. Had this been broadcast back in July 1935, when the matter of examining and reporting on the entire problem of Air Raid Precautions (ARP) became the business of the RAF's Wing Commander Eric Hodsell, CB, and of the ARP Department, it might have met with disbelief from the general public. On the other hand, it might have better prepared them for the 'inevitable' conflict. What the outcome of such a broadcast would have been is pure conjecture.

As it was, some two and a half years later, in December 1937, following the passage of the Air Raid Precautions Act, the news was eventually disseminated, albeit in a dumbed-down manner, via community newsletters, parish magazines and the like. Members of Parliament had already voted in favour of a plan calling for air-raid shelters to be erected in most of Britain's towns and cities, and Winston Churchill told the House of Commons that air-raid shelters 'would be indispensable' and that 'well-organised precautions' would mean that 'air attacks on Britain would not be worthwhile'.

The notes of the local committee in Brockenhurst, Hampshire, adequately sum up the situation and the mood of those times.

> This is the first occasion on which notes on this important matter have appeared in our bulletin. It is proposed that in the future there shall always be some account of recent happenings and progress as well as notes on various aspects of gas warfare and in particular of course, means of combating it. The writer makes no pretence of being an expert but he has had the job of Air Raid Precaution Officer thrust upon him and has in consequence given the subject some thought and made some study of it. No apology will therefore be offered for quoting freely from government publications and from the writing of experts. Opinion thus expressed will indeed have the greater force and authority.

The year 1937 had already been eventful by the time the published plans for Air Raid Precautions began to go the rounds of local authorities and other public bodies.

Away from the corridors of power, most people were carrying on their lives relatively unaffected by world and European events. While it must be recognised that on the streets there were, of course, mumblings about the possibility of war, these seem to have been contained within certain right-wing groups. The so-called working class, on the other hand, was kept in its place with carefully selected drips of information that gave them no reason to be alarmed or to be overly concerned about the prevailing circumstances.

In Aldershot, the traditional home of the British Army, the annual Searchlight Tattoo, which came to symbolise the spirit and patriotism of the pre-war years and which remains legendary in the annals of social and military history, drew tremendous crowds, in excess of 300,000. Ironically, in contrast to the 'entertainment and spectacle' afforded by the events in the Rushmoor Arena, and almost certainly without the knowledge of those who flocked to the Tattoo, the military authorities in the town were preparing for war.

On the world stage, Amelia Earhart, the pioneering aviator, had vanished without trace during a flight in July of that year. Another aviation loss was that of the famous airship *Hindenburg*, which crashed in flames as it docked in New York. On a lighter note, the Walt Disney Studios released *Snow White and the Seven Dwarfs*, the first animated feature film and considered to be a masterpiece of its time. Idealists from many countries were flocking to Spain to fight in the Civil War, and Rheims Cathedral was reopened following its long restoration after the First World War. Also in France, the French Army was firing dummy shells over the local village of Atwiller as part of an exercise to assess the capabilities of the Maginot Line.

Back in Britain, meanwhile, the broadsheet newspapers were advertising the latest Morris 12 motor car, offered with 'splendid acceleration' at the reasonable

A scene from one of the pre-war Aldershot Tattoos. *(Aldershot Military Museum)*

In contrast, a rally held in Germany at about the same time. *(Author's collection)*

price of £205 and with the suggestion that, if you did not buy a Morris, you should at least buy a car made in the United Kingdom. In the same papers, many column inches were given to a report of the speeches by Mussolini in which he said he was ready to help solve Europe's problems. The correspondent who filed the story emphasised that, in one audience alone of some 600,000 people, over 90 per cent were in uniform.

A piece of home news that was eventually to lead to one of the most sensational cases in British criminal history was given less coverage, and in comparison to most other news at the time seemed of no great significance. Bill Neal remembers it very well though.

It was about a chap in the RAF. He was something of a playboy, and I really took an interest in this case because for some time I had wanted to join the Air Force. I dreamed about the day I was doing something worthwhile. I had collected a lot of books about aeroplanes and about flying, and this is what I wanted to do when I was old enough. I had lived near an old First World War airfield in Hampshire and had heard stories from local people, and I had seen photographs taken there. Anyway, I had this perception of how proper and smart RAF people were and didn't think I would fit in. I considered them heroes.

The case I read about in the paper really made me think. '*A pilot officer of the RAF was found not guilty of desertion by a Court Martial sitting yesterday [Friday, 20 August 1937]. He was convicted on two other counts to which he pleaded guilty. The accused officer, 20, of No. 73 Fighter Squadron pleaded not guilty to deserting His Majesty's Forces on March 22, 1937 by absenting himself from the RAF station until apprehended on June 22.*' So who was the officer who boasted of his playboy life-style and somewhat charmed existence? It was none other than Neville George Clevely Heath. He was to hang for the murder of two women, one of whom was attacked near Bournemouth, and it was suspected, although never proven, that he was also responsible for a third murder. He was executed on 16 October 1946. The reason this story and this date are relevant is because it is the same date that sentences were passed on war criminals at the International Tribunal in Nuremberg.

By 1937 the Government's two-year plan to treble the strength of the Royal Air Force was complete. For the Royal Navy, HMS *Ark Royal* was launched during a 'programme of introducing of new vessels', and bonus increases were being made to over 50,000 Admiralty shipyard workers.

The prevailing political situation, which many still either did not understand or consider to be of no threat to the safety of the people of these islands, prompted many letters to the editors of newspapers. In the *Sunday Times* of 5 December 1937 one correspondent from Bournemouth wrote: 'Unless there is a complete change in the mood of Europe, the real front line trenches in the next war will not be in Picardy, but here at home. No preparations can guarantee safety, what can be guaranteed is freedom from panic and such reduction of material damage and such a risk to the attackers as shall make air raids on our towns not worthwhile.' Later in

the same piece, the writer suggested that, 'To face the problems of modern war is to make a next war not more, but less likely. To turn our backs on them is to make it [war] certain.'

In contrast, a contributor from Andover offered this: 'Sirs, I cannot believe that this nation considers war inevitable. Too much talk and barely little published evidence of a real threat takes the mind away from the day to day business of providing for the people through a sound industrial base and employment and a booming export market. Address the situation we know about, not a situation which a hand-ful imagine.'

Neville Heath, former RAF Pilot Officer.
(Police Museum/New Scotland Yard)

However, events in Spain were being seen by an increasing number of 'informed' people as an indication of what might happen in Britain if war came. The bombing of towns and cities caused widespread death and destruction and proved that aerial bombardment, if unchecked, could bring a country to its knees without the need for large invading armies. These events reinforced the beliefs of those who were to push through the provisions of the ARP Act.

And so it was that in late 1937 the call went out for volunteers and experienced persons to fill various posts associated with the tasks to be performed within the

Events in Britain would soon mirror those in Spain when bombing began on the Home Front. (*Author's collection*)

parameters of the Act. Air-raid wardens would operate from designated ARP posts, which were each to be equipped with at least one telephone and staffed by two persons. The Cycle Corps would consist of at least six motorcyclists or pedal cyclists, and they would assume responsibility for the collection and delivery of mail, the handling of dispatches and the carrying of small items of equipment. The Rescue and Demolition Squad would have the harrowing task of clearing up after air raids, although volunteers could always be found for this team. Stretcher-bearers were always needed, and so too were volunteers for the Decontamination Squads.

Nelly Cooke of Petersfield wrote in her diary:

> All this talk of another war, I am not sure if we should be worried or if we should just get on with our daily lives. One good thing is that we are an island and we may have some breathing space before any country considers attacking us. Hopefully we can be robust and deter anyone who threatens us. Anyway, we cannot influence world events and we must be resolute for our children's sake.

Elsewhere in the notes made by Nelly at the time, she records how the local women's group had started to preserve foodstuffs and 'the local menfolk' had begun to make a list of shotguns and pistols for a proposed armoury in their village. Many guns and pistols were souvenirs of the Great War and could be put to 'good use' for home defence.

Two years before the eventual outbreak of war, despite the introduction of the ARP Act – shortly followed by the Fire Brigades Act – opinion still remained divided as to the likelihood of a European or worldwide conflict similar to that of two decades earlier. As one commentator recorded, 'Try as they might, they [the British] never quite succeeded in taking a realistic view of the prospects before them.'

Many were paying lip service to the reality while taking the precautions advised by the Government, making the necessary sacrifices and working like beavers to prepare. They dug trenches, learnt passwords, divided up limited stocks of ammunition, selected sites for mass graves and built shelters. They listened to discouraging reports of German tactics and cleared land for defensive purposes. While they felt they could give a good account of themselves, seemingly they still found it impossible to appreciate the terrible dangers that invasion was expected to throw at them.

Unbeknown to the masses, decisions for war had already been made and it was now just a matter of time.

2

A Programme of Aggression

I think we all knew by 1938 that the oppressive climate in Europe would soon cast its gloom upon us.

(Raymond Elliot writing to a cousin in Canada after the war)

The year 1938 was to witness the first flight by the Empire Air Mail Service, the release of the classic Hitchcock film *The Lady Vanishes* and the launch of the 'Roses' brand of chocolates from Messrs Cadbury & Company. The year was also to witness the Empire Exhibition, which was staged in Glasgow at the staggering cost of £11 million. It attracted over thirteen million people, all of whom were able to marvel at the extravagant celebration of and monument to the art-deco style.

Away from the excitement of the exhibition, the world was continuing to reel from one crisis to another. The German Army invaded Austria in March, and later that same month Neville Chamberlain was clear in his declaration to Czechoslovakia that no guarantee of support could be given by Britain if the invading army turned its attentions to that country. The months rolled on and the road to war was becoming shorter. The Czech Crisis was played out, to the dismay of a watching western world, and the Munich Agreement of September 1938, which was regarded by many as a temporary, albeit welcome, diversion for Britain, would soon prove worthless.

The defence of the nation was now of concern, and the breathing space afforded by the Munich Agreement was seen as the chance to catch up on putting into place all the vital facilities and services that a country at war would need. It was by now recognised that, as and when attack came, it would be primarily from the air. The Fire Brigades Act, as the ARP Act of a year earlier, was to provide for the mobilisation of men and women, the introduction of procedures and protocols, the purchasing or leasing of equipment, premises and vehicles and the issuance of advice and instructions to the civilian population.

Meanwhile, the development of the ARP scheme was very slowly gaining momentum. Bob Tilsley was one of those charged with responsibility for ensuring his Parish Council acted in accordance with Government instructions. He quotes from the Bulletin he put out in January 1938:

Gentlemen, as if to enforce the necessity for Precautions about which we have been previously advised, I now bring to your attention the following which I have received most recently from those who are far more knowledgeable than we. I ask now for your full co-operation and support and please remember, we may only be going through the motions now, however, it may be only a matter of time before this is a real and active situation.

1. Measures for safeguarding the civil population against the effects of air attack have become a necessary part of the defensive organisation of any country which is open to attack. The need for them is not related to any belief that war is imminent. It rises from the fact that the risk of attack from the air is a risk that cannot be ignored.

2. Because preparations to minimise the consequences of attack from the air cannot be improvised on the spur of the moment, they must be made, if they are to be effective, in time of peace.

3. The risk of poison gas being used remains a possibility and cannot be disregarded.

Bob continued by saying, 'You know, looking back, there was almost a casual approach to all this. Some people volunteered immediately, others tended to stroll in, clearly unaware of how vital this activity was.'

We will now take a view of the Air Raid Precautions organisation as a whole, which, despite considerable advertising and requests for help, was not making the progress that was either expected or needed. Many more volunteers would be required, as weaknesses in both manpower and training were beginning to worry those in authority and those whose job it was to recruit.

Despite the earlier announcement that air-raid shelters would be built for the safety of the population, questions were being asked as to why not enough public shelters were being made available. The answer given was blunt. Because warnings of an attack were only made about seven to ten minutes before a raid, the provision of shelters would invite people to congest the streets and expose themselves to attack at the time of greatest danger. Secondly, it was suggested that there would not be enough time for everyone to reach the shelters and, thirdly, the shelters themselves would attract attention as targets for high-explosive bombs. As a postscript to these reasons for the non-provision of enough public shelters, the matter of cost was raised!

By 1939, however, the domestic Anderson shelters were given free of charge to people on incomes of less than £250 per year and to manual workers. To all other non-qualifying people the cost of the shelter was £7. Geoff Burrows, now retired and living in Lee-on-Solent, recalls:

Playing happy families for the camera, this family has taken delivery of an indoor shelter. *(Author's collection)*

When we removed the 'door' that Father had made for the entrance and looked into the shelter, instead of seeing a yellow floor, all we could see was a moving mass of black! The shelter had become home to a colony of devil's coach-horse beetles. Mother screamed and said she would rather be bombed than go in there. Anyway, a covering of borax killed all the beetles, which Father swept up by the shovelful. After that, we kept the iron channels that formed the base edge of the shelter filled with borax, and we were never again invaded by the beetles.

The Morrison shelter, which was introduced the following year, 1940, also cost £7, although this too was free to persons earning less than £350. The £100 difference in the qualifying incomes that had been set previously reflected the changed circumstances of the population and the country at the time.

However, the most popular shelter, which also happened to be free, was the cupboard under the stairs, which many families had in their houses. One obvious advantage was the fact that there was no glass to shatter onto the people gathered inside.

Interestingly, the use of public shelters was not as great as one might imagine.* One woman who lived in Alresford commented, 'I never went in them. They were built everywhere, but we presumed we would have enough time to get home. You never went far from home in the war years.'

Many shops, factories and offices of course had shelter provision for their staff, and schools also had shelters. One former school pupil recalled: 'They were cold and damp and dark for the most part. We used to sing, tell each other stories . . . and pray!'

Training in anti-gas techniques was by now recognised as essential for all ARP personnel, and due attention was paid to providing such training as a priority to

---

* After the war a survey was conducted, yet few of the people questioned could remember where the public shelters had been in their area.

the fire-fighting parties, those involved in rescue and demolition and the decontamination parties. In addition, some specialist teams would be given first-aid training.

The ARP schemes were to be organised on the basis of a system of Air Raid Wardens, each having responsibility for a specific area within the community. Areas were divided into business and residential sectors, each under the charge of a warden.

Mary Weller's husband, Ron, was an ARP Warden.

In the event of a raid, it was the duty of the warden to remain at his post, by the telephone. Anyone living or working near the post who required assistance would contact the warden; meanwhile another ARW was patrolling the area to give assistance to those caught out in the open. When assistance was needed, he

Ready and waiting: members of a civil defence unit 'somewhere in the south of England'. (*Sharon Cross, SHM*)

would contact the post or the local headquarters, and there would be, if the area was up to strength, two reserve wardens to provide further assistance. In the country areas, ARP posts would be placed where it was considered appropriate.

Generally speaking, the job of the ARW was (a) to understand the nature of air warfare, gas, fires and high explosives, (b) to know the organisation of the local ARP scheme, (c) to reconnoitre and report the fall of bombs, the occurrence of fires or the presence of gas, (d) to aid and advise all persons requiring assistance. Finally, it was the responsibility of the warden (f) to prevent panic.

Exercises took place across the county in order to ascertain the likely effect of partial blackouts. Whole areas were subject to lighting restrictions, often during the hours between midnight and 2 a.m. Car headlights were to be used only with the blackout cover fitted, and street lighting was switched off altogether. Aircraft flying overhead would be able to observe how effective the blackouts were. In coastal areas the exercises were also carried out with the participation of the Navy.

Geoff Burrows provides his own perspective:

Father became an air-raid warden, and reported every night to a concrete warden's post erected in a local flowerbed! I would sometimes be sent there with a packet of sandwiches for him, and he and the rest of the wardens would be glad to have somebody to talk to, to break the boredom of waiting for something to happen. In fact Father got fed up and enlisted into the Army early in 1940, so I never got to see the wardens in action. He gave me his blue warden's tin hat when he left. And later it was to save my life.

While some were thinking about possible gas attacks and others were talking about the effects of the blackout, Doreen Bowers, now living in Waterlooville, remembers the family holiday.

The year 1938 was particularly memorable for me. I do remember that year very well because I was going on holiday to Cliftonville with my pal Jean. I was seven years of age, the same age as Princess Margaret, and she got a new bike that year for a present. This was going to be my first holiday away from my family because I was being taken away by Jean's parents. My grandmother was an excellent needlewoman and she agreed to make matching dresses for me and Jean. At the time there was a very popular song called 'Two Little Girls in Blue' and that's what Jean's dad used to call us. Mum bought me a new pair of pyjamas, which was a real novelty. Up till then I only remember wearing pyjamas with holes in.

With new pyjamas, some second-hand shoes (Mum bought six pairs for the same price as one pair of new shoes), new dress and a great big smile on my face, I boarded the paddle steamer at Tower Bridge and we steamed down the

The young Doreen (right) with her brother Frank and sister Beryl. (*D. Bowers*)

Thames to Southend-on-Sea. I never thought then that only a couple of years later whole stretches of the dockland and other sites along the Thames would be gone. At Southend we went on another boat, the *Royal Eagle*, to Margate and from there I think we went by bus to Cliftonville. We were booked into a guest house and had a family room, which meant Jean and I shared a bed. One special memory I have of that week was going to see the Palm Court Orchestra. Jean and I were allowed to stay up late to see them in a special performance, which was being broadcast live for the radio.

To many, the long hot summers of the pre-war era and the fun they had, despite hardship, were halcyon years that are recalled with noticeable fondness and affection.

❖   ❖   ❖

In 1938, the ARP Wardens carried out a survey in respect of the sizes and numbers of gas masks needed in their areas. It was evident from the information fed back to the authorities that not enough provision had been made for the supply of certain sizes. The moulded rubber General Civilian respirator was available in small, medium, large and extra large, and these sizes were thought to cover most needs in the population, except those of people with either facial deformities or hollow temples. The medium- and large-size respirators were in short supply, and it was the responsibility of the Avon Rubber Company to step up production to meet the need. It was only two years earlier that the production of gas masks had been resurrected, based on new designs, and by the end of the war Britain had manufactured some ninety-seven million units.

Tom Foley was eight years old when he was 'introduced' to a gas mask for the first time:

The young children had what became known as Mickey Mouse masks and you could make a rather rude raspberry sound with them. I had a small adult's size mask, although it was rather big on me. It was scary and many of my friends – the boys, not the girls – seemed rather suspicious of them. One of the ladies in the street was elderly and had trouble breathing, so she was given a special mask which you could only get if you provided a medical certificate. It was for people with respiratory problems.

Interestingly, the variant mask for babies, the GC3 or Baby Protector Helmet, was manufactured by several companies, including Messrs Frankenstein & Sons of Manchester – an apt name, perhaps, for a piece of apparatus that was rather frightening, at least to the younger generation.

It was required by law that everyone should carry a gas mask, but after a time, when no gas attacks had arrived, nor did there appear to be a likelihood of any in the future, people tended to get slack and forgot to carry them. Maybe the final word here on gas masks should rest with an elderly lady who was questioned by a colonel who was fire-watching in Portsmouth. 'Madam, where is your gas mask?' The reply: 'Up in my Annie's room behind the clock!'

When Hitler's army invaded Austria in 1938, Winston Churchill was warning Parliament that Europe was confronted with a 'programme of aggression, nicely calculated and timed, unfolding stage by stage'. The reaction to this statement was one of alarm, although it was clear to all that Britain did not have the armaments to resist. In fact, the Chiefs of Staff declared that attacking Germany would be 'like a man attacking a tiger before he has loaded his gun'.

Thus it was that, while the Government's foreign policy was about practising reasonable diplomacy, at home it initiated a major programme of rearming by awarding defence contracts the like of which had never been known before. The John Laing company alone undertook a volume of defence business valued at £7.5 million.

Roger Flear recalled:

A rare photograph of Adolf Hitler in a civilian suit, rather than in his familiar uniform. *(Author's collection)*

Meanwhile, we were trench-digging for air-raid shelters in all the local parks. We drew staff from every other department and from the Labour Exchange. If they could hold a shovel, they could dig a trench. We literally worked around the clock. We arranged meals for the night shifts by phoning Joe Lyons at four o'clock, and they would deliver to the sites. We would do all the wages and would finish taking the packets round by 3.30 in the morning. But we were always back in the office by 8.30 a.m.

The Supply Branch, under the wing of the Office of Works, was endeavouring to discharge its obligations to purchase and distribute, for the civilian population alone, Anderson shelters and fittings and various sizes of gas masks, the combined total of units being over five million. In addition, it was charged with the task of supplying an initial 475,000 sandbags and a list of items which included 1.7 million light anti-gas suits, 20,000 tons of bleach, 1.8 million steel helmets, electric torches, whistles, rattles and hand bells to the civil defence organisations. The final total order for sandbags, to include replacements and items in store, was a staggering 525 million.

Meanwhile, across Britain, matters of daily business were being discharged by local committees; by way of example, it is worth taking a look at one piece of news that was considered worthy of comment in a Hampshire village in April. The chairman of the Parish Council reported that public seats, to be provided out of the Coronation funds (presumably derived one year earlier), had now been constructed, and it was intended to place them in position during the week following the meeting. The report does not mention where the seats were to be sited but indicates that the cost was £20 and that this was taken from Parish funds, which were in credit to the sum of £40.

Norma Loughley recalls:

Looking back, it's difficult to reconcile those times with the great changes in the way of life and the world after 1945. The whole of our lives had changed, the culture, the routine, the expectations, everything was so totally different. For me, 1937 and 1938 were grand years. I was happy, in a great family and we had a weekly treat of going to the cinema, and then for birthdays and special occasions we might be allowed to go skating. I was coming up to twelve years of age and was able to understand and learn more, so I took a lot more in. Father was strict, but it did me, my sister and brother well in the years to come. We seemed to be living two lives, one preparing for war and one believing that we could carry on just as we had done. It was strange and exciting.

We, like everyone else, were to endure great sadness and loss, but we had the confidence from our father, and that helped us through, I am sure.

3

Declaration of War

We listened with mounting excitement and bewilderment as the Prime Minister announced we were at war.

(Doreen Bowers)

As war clouds loomed, the year 1939 became ever more distinct in the minds of everyone. Whether involved with preparations, evacuation or just the day-to-day business of living in uncertain times, people were soon to become aware that, from then on, life would change for ever.

One person who welcomed 1939 in with style was Rose Forbes Wood, who was spending time with family and friends in Connecticut:

We told them of the plans for air-raid shelters and gas masks and the instructions that were being issued to the population about how to do this and that in the event of war. Until we were asked to talk about it, the reality hadn't touched us. When we returned to England in January 1939, it wasn't long before we were totally enveloped in the preparations, and later Father offered part of our house for the Air Raid people.

Young Doreen Bowers was wrapped up in family events that were, in hindsight, to have a somewhat amusing outcome in the prevailing climate of pessimism:

My Aunt Kath's wedding plans were going ahead and I was to be bridesmaid. There were going to be five of us in all, with one lad as the page boy. I can easily remember who the other bridesmaids were. My sister Beryl, my cousin Margaret and my mum's cousins – and their names were May and Daisy. These names were very fashionable at the time. Brian, who was the nephew of Les, the bridegroom, was to be the page boy and Les's brother Ernie was to be best man.

The date of the wedding was fixed for 9 September 1939!

Across the county, civilian respirator cartons were being distributed, to the 'joy' of many local authorities. One clerk recorded, 'At long last the respirators arrived', and, 'The whole consignment of these – 2,400 in number – were assembled by a body of willing workers on Friday and the bulk of them distributed to Air Raid Wardens on Friday afternoon and Saturday morning.'

There appeared now to be a state of limbo in many matters concerning the whole business of civil defence, such that many of those who had already answered the call for volunteers were wondering why there was so little activity. Although many lectures and courses had taken place up until early 1939, activities such as collective training and practices had yet to be fully implemented or undertaken.

Bob Little, a child of the post-war years, has copies of some of his grandfather's writings:

It seems that the reason for this was because many areas, specifically those in the country and in what were regarded for operational purposes as rural areas, were uncertain as to the level of services and manpower they were to provide to meet Home Office objectives. My grandfather had something to do with the raising of volunteers, and his local community had been working on the basis as recorded in his log.

The log indicates that the intentions were to raise thirty-six wardens, four men for the First Aid Party, twelve women fully trained in first aid for the actual First Aid Point, twelve men and women for the Ambulance Service (and they also needed four cars and one lorry) plus twelve men for the Decontamination Squad. For the Communications Section they were intending to get six people, either car drivers or motorcycle riders.

Bob continues: 'They then received instructions from the Home Office, and I am guessing that this is in early 1939, it doesn't say, that personnel and equipment for their area were to be in numbers much lower that those against which they had tried to recruit.'

The instructions issued by the Home Office make fascinating reading, and it is worth quoting from one paper issued in response to questions about the recruitment of sufficient personnel for duties on the Home Front. The postscript of the person communicating this information to his local council is also worthy of note.

The typical conditions in a (rural) parish in which bombs may fall may be pictured as follows. There may be a constable and two or three special constables, who, though having other duties to perform, may be assumed to be available to give assistance if damage is caused by bombs. These men will have the protective equipment issued to the Police. There will be ARWs on the scale of perhaps 3 to every 500 population also in possession of some protective equipment and with a first aid box. There will be a First Aid point with its equipment and one or two trained attendants. These constitute the formal air raid precautions provision.

The writer noted that: 'The organisation fully sanctioned is likely to be some-where between the two, our estimates and the Home Office requirements. However, until this organisation is known, there is little that can suitably be done except mark time. There is no point in trying to complete or train an organisation which ultimately may not be sanctioned.'

It must be remembered that, although many so-called rural areas were designated as reception sites for evacuees, there was already a building programme under way for the construction of storage facilities, Ack-Ack sites and various military installations in villages large and small. Therefore such an influx of civilians and military personnel would make every location a high-risk target.

As the year 1939 marched on, many local communities were at last receiving approval from the local and county councils for their district ARP schemes, attached to which would now be an agreed number of personnel to cover all activities, including first aid and Rescue and Demolition Squads. However, the worrying news was that many of the previously recruited individuals had not yet received the training or experience through mock exercise that the Home Office was expecting. Indeed, the local communities were concerned that, when war came, as it inevitably now would, there was likely to be a less than beneficial response from the emergency teams.

That said, public meetings were being arranged at which various speakers were to give a good account of the preparations needed, the role of the ARP and the role expected of householders in emergency situations. One member of each household was expected to attend the meetings, during which 'films depicting air raids' were shown, as were films about first-aid practice. Attendance at these meetings by members of the fire services was common, to demonstrate and display fire-fighting practices.

To put things into perspective, the Government had a mammoth task on its hands, which it was trying to accomplish effectively while maintaining the output of industry and farming and the balance of daily life. In addition to the introduction of the ARP, the strengthening of the services (both civilian and military), the building of airfields and military installations and the planning for evacuation, other tasks of equal

A typical pre-war Leyland fire appliance, one of the types brought into wartime service. *(Author's collection)*

priority, such as rationing, the supply of oil from overseas and the mobilisation of thousands of men and women for war work, needed to continue apace, and without causing the population as a whole to panic.

The issuing of whistles to Air Raid Wardens was now being undertaken, although in some more vulnerable areas rattles and hand bells would be used instead. For the princely sum of 6*d*, the owners and operators of cars could purchase ARP Handbook number 4, which explained how to decontaminate vehicles (and properties) after a gas attack. The War Office meanwhile was putting out the call for more volunteers to join the Territorial Army to bring it up to 'war establishment' strength.

Charlie Bifield fondly recalls the year 1939, because it held a special memory for him.

It was a memorable year for me in more ways than one. Of course war was declared late in the year, but more importantly for me, I married my fiancée Eva in 1939. I was fully expecting to be receiving my call-up papers then, but in fact it wasn't until a few months later that I was eventually conscripted and I joined the RAF.

For Pamela Spurrier, the year was memorable for different reasons.

I was one of six children. Mum was a widow because my father had died when I was just four years old. Life was harder in those days for single parents and times really were getting more difficult daily. Unfortunately, Mum was forced to let four of the children go into an orphanage.

It was very heartbreaking for all of us. It was I, my younger sister Rosie and my two brothers Jim and Charlie who were taken in by the National Children's Home. I remember we were issued with gas masks and trained how to use them. I didn't like them one little bit. It was the smell and the rubber itself. It just added to the feeling of unhappiness. We had to use the masks of course, and carry them with us at all times.

Len Lewis, another member of the immediate pre-war generation, recalls:

My earliest memories of the second war began in Portsmouth. I can just about remember one afternoon when everybody was staring up into the sky and looking at what they said was a German aircraft. This must have been just before the war began, and the plane turned out to be taking photographs of the Royal Dockyard in preparation for bombing raids when the war started.

We were all issued with gas masks, from babies to the elderly. I seem to remember that the babies' gas masks were a huge version of the adult mask, and

The young James Spurrier (left) with his brothers. *(J. Spurrier)*

they were laced up at the back after the baby was put inside. The poor things seemed very trapped inside. I can remember my mum and her neighbour trying to work out how to lace it up after they had put my baby brother inside. The thing was laid on the dining table and I could see him through the gas-mask window bawling his eyes out. He was obviously very frightened. I started crying too, because I thought he could not breathe.

As I was four years old at the time, I had a small child's version, which had a rubber vent and this made a rude noise every time you breathed through it. Most of the boys would see who could blow the loudest raspberry sound.

As the political climate intensified, so too did the seriousness with which training of all the emergency services was implemented. By mid-1939 more and more volunteers were passing out from courses, including first aid, rescue and fire-fighting. More vehicles were now being commandeered to be used as ambulances or fire tenders and for other emergency purposes.

As if by way of compensation to offset this frenetic activity, the country was enjoying fine weather, with average daily temperatures of 55°F, and a high of 87°F on the hottest day. Across the North Sea, Germany was also enjoying fine weather with similar temperatures. The café society of Berlin, Munich, Frankfurt and other cities was basking in the belief that times were perfect, all was in order and the impending war would merely be a short-lived and decisive formality towards achieving the status Hitler had declared that the nation rightly deserved.

Jim Kelly recalls:

Those pre-war and early war years always seemed to be hot and bright and we spent a lot of time on the beach. When the war came it was difficult to reconcile the wonderful summer weather and the killing that was going on in the skies during the Battle of Britain. We always associate summer with pleasure and enjoyment. It was certainly nothing like that for all those lads who were being shot out of the summer skies and into the warm summer sea.

Joan Stockdale adds her memories:

At the outbreak of war I was teaching people to ride. I lived in Romsey and this was at a time when I was convalescing from an illness, so my capacity was very much reduced and I was not fit enough to join up. I remember that, like almost everyone else, I spent some time filling sandbags, a back-breaking but very necessary task.

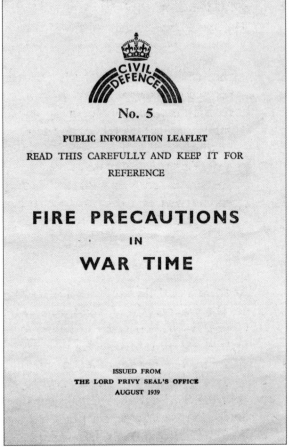

I was a tally clerk supporting the Timber Corps. It was my job to keep track of production and demand for supply of timber for use by industry and, of course, for the war effort. Later, I was given a Green Card, which allowed me to go for an interview with the First Aid Nursing Yeomanry. I never pursued this but my father supported my wish to return to the reserved occupation, and when I did, I also joined the local detachment of the Red Cross.

The Rescue and Demolition Squads of the ARP were now divided into two units, called Heavy and Light, with the Light Unit consisting of ten men, to include one foreman and three 'skilled' men, the remaining six members of the unit having responsibility for 'general

One of the many pamphlets issued to the public. *(Author's collection)*

assistance'. Four members of the party would be trained in first aid in case the actual first-aid team was not immediately available. The Heavy Unit would be held in reserve to deal with incidents that were extremely difficult and extensive in nature.

By now, ARP Handbook number 12 could be purchased for just 3*d*, and this addressed the issue of animals and how to safeguard them during raids. The welfare of humans was, of course, also a priority, and a newly issued leaflet from the Ministry of Food gave this helpful advice for the 'welfare' of the spirit:

> Try to make soup every day so that you always have some to heat up in an emergency. A hot drink works wonders for the nerves at a time of shock or strain. After a shock, the blood pressure and temperature of the body tend to fall. A hot drink, if only hot water, helps to restore them and prevent that sick, faint feeling. Nothing could be better than hot vegetable soup, as this is nourishing as well as soothing.

Coincidentally, in 1939, Bourneville Cocoa, perhaps one of the 'hot drinks' suggested by the Ministry of Food, had been reduced in price!

In Britain's High Streets, the word 'patriotism' was being more widely used in advertising home-produced goods. Use of the word had a double meaning, in that it boosted the morale and endorsed the need to 'buy British' to ensure the factories remained in full production. Later, when many industrial plants were requisitioned for war work, the 'buy British' slogans were replaced by 'support Britain', which amounted to the same thing.

Cocoa, perhaps one of the hot drinks recommended by the Ministry of Food. *(Cadbury Schweppes plc)*

WVS recruiting buses were used to encourage volunteers to enlist. *(WRVS)*

The frenzy of preparation for war continued apace, and across the land private houses were being requisitioned for use by the civilian and military services. Near the Hampshire coast it was noted that plans were well advanced for most eventualities. For example, Setley House at Boldre, near Lymington, was identified for use as a hospital both for evacuees and for those suffering from minor infectious diseases. Boldre Grange was to be used for evacuees, while Langley Hall at Colbury was to be an isolation hospital. There was to be a sick bay at Bench View, Lyndhurst, and First Aid Posts at Hythe, Fawley and Brockenhurst.

The ranks of the Women's Voluntary Service (WVS) had expanded and were reaching 150,000 members. The volunteers were drawn from groups who, for one reason or another, were unable to join up for essential war work. These were older people, the housebound and those with dependants. Interestingly, men were not excluded, and occasionally they assisted with vital tasks such as driving, because not many women could drive at the time.

In the months before the declaration of war, large construction companies, including John Laing, were providing the Government with details of their capabilities in terms of the manpower and equipment at their disposal. These companies had been building military installations for the War Department since the mid-1930s and were probably more aware than most of the inevitability of war in Europe. Laing was able to report that 4,000 men would be available in an emergency, together with 21 horse-drawn vehicles, 12 cranes, 29 pumps and 136,000 yards of scaffolding. In addition, it could make available 75 concrete mixers, 11 lorries (including 6 new Bedfords with trailers) and last, but not least, 1 Ford box van.

One of many work teams from John Laing engaged on airfield construction. *(J. Laing)*

Almost all construction companies made teams available to respond to emergencies such as air raids. Laing was no exception and it agreed immediately to keep ten men on 24-hour standby, with ten vehicles for demolition and decontamination work.

With the continuing emphasis on ARP and the building of air-raid shelters, it was now time to focus the public's attention on the warning signals that were to be given prior to and after air raids. Wardens would give sharp blasts on a whistle to alert everyone to the fact that a raid was likely in five to ten minutes. If a gas attack was likely, hand rattles would be used instead, and a hand bell would then be used as an 'all clear' to signal the cancellation of the gas warning or 'raiders passed and no gas'. These manual signals would be given when sirens were not operational in, for example, rural areas and areas not considered sufficiently important enough to warrant the installation of a proper siren!

In addition to the advice about following the signals given by the wardens, members of the public were further instructed to take shelter or cover immediately a warning was heard. 'If one behaves sensibly,' said Catherine Thomas, reading from a leaflet she has kept safely in her scrap book, 'the only real danger is from a direct hit. First, if you lie down flat in the smallest hollow, in an open space – perhaps a hollow you hardly noticed when standing up – you are safe from everything except a direct hit and the slight danger from anti-aircraft shell fragments. Second, you can hear bombs coming, therefore if you hear them while running for shelter, don't run. Drop where you are.'

The advice given continues in the same 'amusing' way. 'It's very probable that gas will be used. Prepare for gas, then laugh at it, but prepare for it. Flying glass is one of the greatest dangers in an air raid. Never therefore hang about behind glass windows. Don't throw water on to burning incendiary bombs.' The first radio broadcast containing hints to householders about improvising air-raid shelters in the home was made on 23 September 1939.

Evacuation began in early September 1939. Notes made by a teacher who was to look after the educational needs of young evacuees vividly describe the experience of all those caught up in the mass exodus from town to country. For them, perhaps more than any other section of the community, it was truly a journey into the unknown. Eric Gadd wrote:

> With a heavy heart, I slammed the front door behind us. When would we again cross that welcoming threshold? Ever?
>
> My wife Daisy and I had risen at four in the morning to set about the many last-minute tasks we knew we would have to attend to following our preparations yesterday. At half past four, we woke the children, who, sleepy-eyed and bewildered, ate what might be their last meal in our home.
>
> Then out into the twilight and off down the hill to the meeting place. Daisy and Mavis, our daughter of six years, carried the hand luggage and gas masks in their cardboard containers. I had one gas mask slung over each shoulder and in my left hand I carried a suitcase. My right arm supported Wendy, our two-year-old, who clutched her teddy bear, her head nestling drowsily on my shoulder.

Eric and his family made their way to a rendezvous point at the Southampton school where he had been teaching. There he met colleagues who were to take pupils to a 'safer' area out of the city and away from the likely targets of enemy bombers. After checking that gas masks and identity labels were in place and all belongings and food needs were accounted for, the party bid a silent farewell to their school and to the many sad-eyed parents who had gathered in the street. Eric went on to describe the tram ride to the station, the long wait in the yard and eventually the train journey. Finally, he noted: 'By nightfall, thanks to superb work by the WVS and their helpers, homes had been found for all the children. I was watching the last of the evacuees being taken off, scared and silent in twos and threes.'

Within a day or so of the start of the evacuation, the announcement of war was broadcast to a nation that by now was as prepared as it ever would be in mind, body and spirit. As for the practical readiness – well, it was getting there, but it actually fell far short of the expectations of those who were involved in safeguarding the population and dealing with the terror that this war was about to unleash. As one commentator said at the time, 'If Mr Hitler concentrates his attentions and his mighty forces in our direction, we must realise that we cannot be a David against his

A poignant scene of the evacuation of children. (*Author's collection*)

Meanwhile in Germany, Hitler acknowledges a crowd of supporters from the window of a dining room. (*Author's collection*)

fearful Goliath. No amount of force on our part will even dent the German war machine.'

The WVS helped to organise and evacuate a total of 1.5 million women and children from the major cities to the country. Children less than five years of age were taken to one of three receiving nurseries, where they had their heads washed and were given any clothes they lacked, before being escorted to country nurseries. In two years 30,000 children were evacuated from the cities. Meanwhile, other members of the WVS were staffing hostels, sick bays and communal feeding centres called British Restaurants.

Doreen Bowers remembers that, after Neville Chamberlain's broadcast announcing Britain's entry into the war, the sirens began to wail and the bells began to ring.

Well, we all thought there was going to be a gas attack so we put on our masks, which had only been issued to us the month before. We sat there for some time until someone came to tell us that it was a false alarm. The church bells did not ring again until the end of the war. Of course, we were to hear the sirens many times during the next five years.

My father, who had been pronounced unfit to be conscripted, had joined the Decontamination Squad and he had been issued a special gas mask. He was attending exercises when he had to enter a gas-filled building for so many seconds without a mask. At school, too, we had regular gas-mask drill.

The Government had already evacuated many children, and several from here had gone to stay with relatives. It was a sad day indeed when Jean said she was going to Norfolk with her cousins and her grandmother. No one realised we would not see her again for five years. Reluctantly, my parents decided that Mum, sister Beryl, brother Frank and I should go to stay with my aunt and uncle in Ringwood until such time as the immediate danger had passed.

The wedding of Aunty Kath to her fiancé Les was scheduled for 9 September. The wedding did go ahead but there were now only two bridesmaids and the page boy. Their prize of a honeymoon in France, which they had won in a competition at a dog track, was cancelled, although the promoter said he would honour the prize when the war was over. I think a lot of people did not imagine that the war would take five years before it ended. The promoter never did honour the agreement!

The evacuation process was tinged with excitement and sadness.

We said a sad farewell to my dad, who had to stay behind because of the work he was doing, and we boarded a very crowded train. There were a lot of service personnel and other evacuated families. Frank and I found the experience very exciting, and because it was a corridor train we spent much of the time looking out of the window. Later, more families boarded the train and I remember two children came and stood by us. We had been peeling an orange that Mum had given us for the journey and these two children snatched the peel and started to eat it. That's the first time we realised that not all children had enough to eat.

We eventually arrived at Ringwood station – which no longer exists by the way – and we must have looked a pathetic group really. Mum trying to carry a very large suitcase, with my sister asleep in her arms and Frank and me tired after the journey. We found our way out of the station and into the High Street and began the walk to Gravel Lane, which was where we were going to stay. A car then drew up alongside our group and a young chap asked us where we were going. Mum replied that we were going to Gravel Lane and by coincidence, this chap was an insurance agent who was going to visit my aunt and uncle. How grateful we all were for that lift!

As Doreen and many other youngsters and mums were being 'uprooted' from their own environments, members of the Civil Defence, that is, all the emergency service volunteers, whose numbers by now had reached sufficient levels for the organisation as a whole to be effective in the event of attack from the air, received a special communiqué from His Majesty, King George VI. Apart from its value in boosting morale, it added considerable weight to the case for being prepared! The King, through the Secretary of State, said:

Now the emergency has come I wish to express to all the Civil Defence Volunteers my appreciation of the way they have responded to the cause and of the fine spirit in which they are facing the long hours and discomfort inseparable from the performance of their duties.

The Queen and I have seen for ourselves something of your organisation and we have no doubt whatever that the courage of the volunteers coupled with patience during times of inaction will be equal to whatever task may be in store for them.

4

Dig for Victory

They made soup and sandwiches for the shipwrecked sailors who came there after rescue.

(Geoff Burrows)

The brilliant weeks of a late summer stretched into September of 1939. While some watched the blue skies in anticipation of seeing Nazi bombers, others were content with playing on the beach, enjoying walks in the countryside and generally trying not to let the reality of war deflect them from carrying on as normal. Who could blame them for trying to overlook the fact that blackouts were in force, gas masks and identity cards had to be carried at all times and a deluge of poster advertising included the advice to 'Dig for Victory', 'Leave the Children where they are' and 'Be like Dad – Keep Mum'?

Rationing – first of petrol – was soon extended to food and other commodities. Glistening barrage balloons were hovering over the towns and cities, and millions of bags were being filled with sand. Tens of thousands of married women were taking on jobs in shops and factories, and the call-up for service personnel accelerated. The Phoney War created an uncomfortable aura of unreality. In everybody's mind now was the thought 'When will they strike?'

Ann Parnaby of Bournemouth was six years old at the beginning of the war, so it was to be memorable for more than one reason:

I think many children had already been evacuated and mother and father (Hilda and Jack) made arrangements with a family in the country to take me in. It was a private arrangement, you might say, because they wanted to ensure that I was going to be perhaps a bit better off than the children who were simply going off to be boarded with strangers in places of which they had no previous knowledge. It

must have been quite frightening for many of them, but I was lucky to be able to stay with people I knew.

Dad was working for Matsui, a Japanese company based in the City, and he used to go off to work in a suit and bowler hat. He was thirty-nine years of age and was not called up, although he did join the ARP and soon became what they called an Incendiary Officer, dealing with the fire bombs. Dad had seen service in the Great War as a soldier with the Queen Victoria Rifles, so he had received military training and was able to make a significant contribution to the emergency services.

Ann settled well into the life of an evacuee and recalls:

I settled in OK really, because we were away from the bombing and the 'real war', if you like, and at six or seven I was still at an age when everything was exciting. We used to scare rats in a nearby barn by pulling open the doors suddenly and watching them run away. I used to help on a milk round. We used to travel around on a cart which was fitted with a huge churn. People would leave jugs and pots out for the milk and I would use a ladle to measure out a pint or quart or a gill. I made lots of friends, although shortly after starting school I was transferred to a private tutor who lived three bus rides away. The authorities said that, because my parents had made private arrangements for me to evacuate, I was not entitled to go to the local village school. Eventually, after pressure from my father, the authorities changed their minds and I returned to the proper school.

Christmas 1939 was the last time that many would celebrate with family and friends. Food was still plentiful in some shops, and choice was not restricted other than by ration. With Christmas came the added dimension of so many people being away from home and in need of comforts, and this applied not only to those evacuees who were still boarded in areas out of harm's way but also to the troops who had taken up 'action stations' in new and existing military establishments across the country. It was to the Church that many looked for the provision of glad tidings, in the practical sense as well as in the spiritual sense.

Notes in a parish magazine produced by the Revd Henry Bridges from a community 'somewhere in the south of England' were typical of the prevailing willingness to 'pull together' and 'help thy neighbour'. In writing about the Christmas party, Mr Bridges says:

The cost of the party is usually about £1 and it was decided to give this amount to be spent on providing Christmas enjoyment for our guests, the troops stationed here to help to protect us. It was felt that this would be the wish of the members if they could all have been consulted. The money has been given to the Officer in Charge and will be added to the fund the men themselves have raised to provide Christmas treats when they can get leave off. . . . The best way in which you can help is by contributing to that fund. I visit the camp each week and shall be pleased to hand over any contributions sent to me for that purpose.

Elsewhere in Hampshire, as in the rest of the country, the Christmas season was a time to concentrate the minds of 'ordinary folk' on the need for more assistance with all sorts of activities which would 'help our men when they are most in need'.

Typically, local groups, or work parties as they were known, supported hospitals and Red Cross depots by undertaking a variety of repairs to materials and by sewing or knitting items such as bed jackets, nightshirts, hot-water-bottle covers and bed socks. Everyone attending a work-party session was expected to bring along 'thimble, needles, cotton and scissors' and was encouraged, if encouragement was ever needed, with the slogan 'Every stitch will help a wounded man'.

These first months of the so-called Phoney War were, nonetheless, a time of considerable tension and sacrifice for many, and there was nothing phoney about the events on mainland Europe. One commentator, with an optimism similar to that voiced at the outbreak of the Great War, was to say: 'We enter the New Year, 1940, with confidence and hope, determined to see the quick end of this ghastly business.' Of course, the 'ghastly business' was to evaporate millions of lives and was to have a lasting impact on all those, of every age, who endured it for six years.

Charlie Bifield remembers:

In March 1940, I went for a medical in the local Drill Hall and it was very cold and the only heating appeared to be a small, old-fashioned oil stove. After the medical, I was interviewed by a naval officer because I expressed the wish to go into the Navy. I then had a test for joining as an Electrical Artificer and I passed this with no trouble. I was then told I would have to join for six years, which surprised me as I thought it would only be for the duration of the war! So I changed my mind and joined the RAF instead. Of course, the war lasted for six years so it made no difference in the end.

Watched by a local family, this 'Tommy' from a nearby camp pauses for a morale-boosting propaganda photograph. *(Private collection)*

For some, however, it was to change their lives in a positive way. Betty Hockey of Bournemouth recalls the period of the Phoney War with affection. It was to be the start of a career in show business, and to this day, she never regrets one moment of her time as a dancer in a concert party.

When war was declared, I moved back to Bournemouth with my small child and moved in with my parents. The family car was shortly thereafter signed over to the Fire Brigade, who were commandeering and making urgent appeals for vehicles at that vital time. I worked in an Army Record Office* in Dunholme Manor on the East Cliff of Bournemouth for a while. Most of the hotels along that area of the coast were eventually taken over by the military.

Betty served in the Record Office for only a short time, because, as she remembers:

It was while I was at the Record Office that a major who had just returned from service in India decided to form a concert party to help raise the morale of the soldiers and other military personnel in the local area. So it was then that I became a 'volunteer' member of a concert party, which was a wonderful new experience.

It gave me the chance to taste, and experience, the show business life even if it was not the West End! My dancing skills were almost non-existent, but I quickly learnt to get by. After a while I decided that the indoor job was not for me. Anyway, by then I had been offered a job driving a small van around the countryside, collecting old tyres which would later go for retreading.

I would drive this van around the 50-mile radius of Bournemouth. Coincidentally, this area was almost the same as the military's Southern Command area, so it made sense to me to start up a concert party of my own. Because of the driving job I was able to drop in to any garrison, camp unit or shore base on my way and book dates for the concert party to visit. I was welcomed with open arms and never once refused.

The concert party was started through an advert in the local paper. Betty continues:

I actually found so many 'artistes', as they were called, were only too pleased to offer their services, even though every one of them, like me, had a full daytime war job. I was quite overwhelmed and so I arranged an audition. With so many talented people to choose from, I ended with a concert party much larger than the average, and also larger than the average ENSA show.

We had a comedian, a comedienne, a tenor and a soprano. We also had a husband and wife who played the xylophone and accordion, we had a

---

* The offices of the Pioneer and Intelligence Corps.

ventriloquist and a magician, a cartoonist, a monologist, and last but not least, a pianist and four dancers. In addition there was the all-important compère, whom we dubbed 'the Baron' because he wore a monocle, and we were also very fortunate to have our own electrician who ably fitted us out with our own lighting run by a petrol-driven generator. This meant, of course, that we could give outdoor shows at will.

How did Betty and the team manage to fit this into the working day?

We would finish our daily work around 5.30 p.m., then travel by our four-car convoy to the units where we gave the shows. Sometimes we did not get back until the early hours, but each of us would be at our job the following morning by 8.30 am. Never once did any of us fail to turn up for work, nor did we ever fail to provide a show at a camp or unit. It was our job to entertain the forces and keep up their morale, and that we did to the best of our ability.

Of course it was important to have a name for the troupe and, as Betty says, 'Both by name and by the hours we put in, we were known as the Non Stops!'

Betty, fourth from left, with other members of the Non Stops. The troupe had performed a show for sailors on a warship moored somewhere off the south coast, 1944. (B. Hockey)

Betty today. She still maintains strong links with the Royal Navy and Army through her work with veterans. *(B. Hockey)*

❖ ❖ ❖

At the dawn of 1940 debate continued about the plight of evacuees in some areas, and it was noted that many, particularly boys, were complaining of being bored. That was certainly true for some who had left the busy streets and home-made 'playgrounds' of the towns and cities to find themselves in what the adults would call an idyllic countryside. While one Colonel C. Mansell-Jones (retired) was to call it a scandal, others involved in the care of evacuated children were to express amazement at how well they had settled down and adapted to their new surroundings.

Eric Gadd, a Hampshire schoolteacher, wrote: 'Over 60 per cent of the evacuated children have joined the Boy Scouts, Girl Guides or similar organisations,' and, 'A considerable number have found outlets for their activity . . . in the busy life of farms, for example.' However, the change in environment was just as much an education for those taking in the children as it was for the evacuees themselves.

Schoolchildren pose anxiously before evacuation. *(Sharon Cross, SHM)*

Conversely, Ann Parnaby recalls the case of one 'foster-mum' who was both surprised and saddened by the children she looked after.

They were two young lads, the Wood brothers from Liverpool, and the foster-mum found it upsetting when she discovered the lads had their clothes all sewn together. The jackets sewn into the pullovers, the pullovers sewn into the vests, with the trousers sewn into the underpants. No one knew when they had last had a change of clothes and whether the clothes had been sewn together to stop them from being taken off the children. After the children were bathed and put to bed, the foster-mum peeped in on them to make sure they were both OK. The lads were not in bed, and upon investigation she found them rolled up in the carpet and lying under the bed.

She asked why they were sleeping under the bed and was told that 'Mum and Dad sleep in the bed, we sleep underneath, and that's what we do at home'. It was assumed they perhaps came from one-room accommodation and had other family members sharing. It was very sad, in any event.

Joan Coup of New Milton adds her experiences. At just eight years of age, Joan was no different from the millions of other youngsters totally unprepared for the change that was about to take place in her life. A quiet little girl, Joan was in the 'second wave' of evacuation a few months after the start of hostilities, when the local authority decided that mums and children of a certain age should be sent to places of safety.

Actually, my mother refused to be evacuated, and because my brother was too young to leave my mother at that time, I was to be sent away on my own.

I remember vividly the day of departure. All the children were waiting in little groups for the coaches to arrive. Last-minute farewells were being said to parents and friends and neighbours. There were, of course, lots of tears and people hugging and apprehensive laughter. There were screams and struggles from those who definitely did not want to go. The scene was no doubt similar to scenes across the country, we children with labels tied firmly into our button-holes and our little paper bags containing food for the journey. Larger luggage had been placed in the boot of the coach.

The journey itself – well, I remember little about that, although I do remember being tearful and being comforted by one of the teachers who was travelling with us. There were to be a few more upsets during the coming weeks, but I am sure that was true of everyone. Making new friends on the train I think helped pass the time and quell the tears. Looking out of the window was another great game.

The new experiences continued as Joan arrived at her destination.

All of it was a new experience, of course, and when we were shown into the village hall we were met by a sea of faces of all the people who had agreed to

A happy evacuee, Joan, with her wartime foster-parents. *(J. Coup)*

take in a child. There was a complete hush as we children gazed at the adults and they gazed at us, but after a few 'hellos' all was back to normal.

We were asked to sit down and be 'good boys and girls' while drinks and biscuits were passed round. My name was eventually called and I met my new 'foster parents' Auntie Flo and Uncle Sam (Mr and Mrs Petherick) for the first time. Apparently Auntie Flo had been watching me for some time while I sat on the floor and counted the pennies that kind friends and neighbours had given me because I was 'going away on holiday'.

Doreen Bowers again:

Arrangements were hurriedly made for Beryl and me to be evacuated under the Government scheme, and so within days we had to report to a local school with our gas masks and luggage, identity labels attached to our coats. As my mother signed us in, the siren wailed and we were ushered into the shelter in a bricked-off part of the school.

Eventually we were summoned to join the buses, which had lined up outside. Our names were checked and we said goodbye to our mums. I was too exited to be upset, although very apprehensive, because this was my first time away from home. When we got to the railway station there were many children, and along the way we picked up more. There was an adult volunteer put in charge of each group of children. At one station there were people on the platform with refreshments and they were handed to us through the carriage windows. I remember drinking a welcome glass of cold milk.

Chris Lewis:

Three of my sisters joined the Army, in the Women's Auxiliary Territorial Service (ATS). One of them became a secretary/typist, one became a driver and the other was part of an anti-aircraft gun team. All my sisters later married soldiers they met during or just after the war, so you can imagine that our house got very crowded at times.

Geoff Burrows:

Mother and Grandmother became volunteer helpers at the local Mission to Seamen. There they made soup and sandwiches for the shipwrecked sailors who came there after rescue. The woman in charge seemed an old harridan, and told Mother off if she put too much margarine on the sandwiches. I suppose she had to spin it out as far as possible, but it seemed hard at the time. I used to go to help, washing dishes and collecting them from the tables. So of course I used to chat to the sailors. Apparently they were forced to take the next available berth on the next ship to sail or face jail! I spoke one day to a sailor who had been torpedoed three times in succession. Everything that he owned was at the bottom of the sea, and he was sailing on another ship the next day.

It was an awful, but very exciting time.

5

Building for a Nation at War

It was vital to keep production rolling and output to a maximum, both on the many construction sites and in the nation's factories.

(Robert Ellery)

In the immediate pre-war years contracts were issued for the building of many facilities, including airfields, barrage-balloon posts and military installations. Under the most strenuous of living and working conditions, following the outbreak of war a vast programme of construction was undertaken, that was to peak with the building of the Mulberry Harbour. And there was song and laughter to keep the morale high.

Throughout the six years of war, the Air Ministry required a great deal of building and civil engineering work so as to meet commitments to the Royal Air Force in its duties at home. In September 1939 several large aerodromes of a 'very substantial' class of construction were nearing completion. These were the first aerodromes forming part of the Royal Air Force Expansion Scheme of the interwar period. When war was declared, the sites were subject to considerable extension, including the building of additional barrack blocks, bomb stores, wireless stations and other ancillary units.

During the eventful days of the Second World War, building and engineering work progressed at a steady pace, with the construction of aerodromes, camps, factories and other vital works throughout the country. Building and civil engineering companies both large and small were called upon by the Government to undertake many difficult and hazardous tasks. Impending operations of vital military importance demanded the ultimate in effort, efficiency and reliability in all needs for and types of construction. Outstanding feats of building and engineering work were accomplished in preparation for the 'final assault' that led to ultimate victory and the end of the war in Europe.

In the early months of 1939 representatives of John Laing* & Son were requested by the Air Ministry at very short notice to undertake the layout, organisation and construction of seven main barrage-balloon depots for occupation within just seven months. Although the company had many other contracts in progress at the time, it was able to complete the Ministry's request within the period, and in fact completed four other similar contracts later in the same year.

One of the first buildings in the construction programme was the headquarters of Bomber Command. As with virtually every other major contract for war build, it was a matter of great urgency to complete the work and have the site operational as quickly as possible. Manpower was thrown at the work, and round-the-clock shifts were necessary to achieve the needed results.

Robert Ellery, who worked as a subcontractor on more than one Government contract in the county, remembers:

Almost overnight I went from peacetime work to the shifts on big contracts which all the workers knew to be essential if we were to build the places for the war effort. Yes, it was very hard work, but then you slept well when you were on

Delivery of more aggregate at a construction site. (J. Laing)

---

* John Laing was already a knowledgeable member of the ARP Committee, and well versed in the need for substantial air defences against enemy bombing of the population.

rest and it was a mix of one's own stamina and knowing that you were helping the country that kept you going. Spirits were high, there was a lot of camaraderie and lots of new friends to make. The construction gangs were quite often under a lot of pressure and were still building places when the military moved in and began their work.

I suppose that was particularly true when we built airfields. The planes used to arrive with personnel and began making sorties even before the runways were fully completed. They were desperate times, and yet we managed to do the job, get the work done and make sure that the places were built to the best standard for the purpose.

Although everything seemed to be done at double-quick pace, the workmanship was always high. You can tell that by the fact some of the buildings are still standing to this day. It's a shame so many were knocked down, because they are reminders of our heritage, and some designs and structures incorporated features ahead of their time really.

It was vital to keep production rolling and output to a maximum, both on the many construction sites and in the nation's factories.

The welfare of the workers and the need to keep morale high were not lost on those in Government, who were, shall we say, far-sighted and aware of the 'psyche' and spirit of the people. Morale-boosting propaganda was not new, and was already being used to noticeable effect from 1939. However, it was not until 1941, when a revolutionary new show was introduced and broadcast by the BBC Home Service, that boosting morale was to achieve tremendous success.*

The radio programme *Workers' Playtime* became an integral part of morale-boosting for those engaged in vital war work. Famous names of the time, including Wilfred Pickles, Elsie and Doris Waters and Charlie Chester, appeared live on stage in many canteens. Another star, Betty Driver,† who is still popular today, recalls: 'I used to sing to entertain the people who went in to some of the underground shelters to sleep.'

The simple music and comedy show was planned and organised with painstaking effort and was broadcast live, but the stars and the location from which it was broadcast remained secret. From 'Somewhere in Britain' groups of variety artists would entertain the workers over the lunchtime period. Barbara Rice recalls:

---

* It was proven to have had a positive effect on the achievements of British workers during the war years.

† Betty Driver is best known for playing the role of the barmaid Betty Turpin in *Coronation Street*.

The young Betty Driver in the early days of her career. (B. Driver)

I'LL WALK ALONE

Words by SAMMY CAHN   Music by JULE STYNE

Featured & Broadcast by BETTY DRIVER

BRADBURY WOOD LTD
MUSIC PUBLISHERS
142 CHARING CROSS ROAD
LONDON, W.C.2
For the United Kingdom of Great Britain and Ireland

MAYFAIR MUSIC CORP., N.Y.

BW 7094

1/- NET

Authorised for sale only in the British Empire (except Canada, Newfoundland and the Continent of Europe)
MADE IN ENGLAND

The acts, whoever they were, always had a wonderful rousing reception from a very enthusiastic audience. I think our canteen in Southampton held about 800 people, and a temporary stage was set up in the best position so we could all see the acts. The people on stage, who were regarded as stars or celebrities, were doing their bit for the war effort, helping to boost morale and lift our spirits. We were all coming together, workers and stars united, to get through the war and to forget the hardships. Many of my friends were widows or had lost a child or family member. But we all pulled through and managed great smiles.

I don't know what we would have done without *Workers' Playtime*. It was one of

A works canteen typical of those from which *Workers' Playtime* was broadcast. (J. Laing)

the best things to come out of the war. The show would travel the length and breadth of the country to factories chosen by the Ministry of Labour. From time to time Ernest Bevan, the Minister for Labour and National Service, would appear on the programme to congratulate the workers and to enthuse them to greater efforts.

Betty Driver recalls:

I had some really great times and met all the stars. Beryl Reid used to be on a lot of the shows with me. The atmosphere in the factories and other places where we broadcast was great. The programme used to go out in all the lunch breaks, and if by any chance the sirens went during the performance the whole of the audience used to disappear into the shelters. I even did a broadcast on a submarine, but you were never told of the location. The people during the war were so great, and we didn't care how long we had to entertain them.

While John Laing & Son made a significant contribution to general building and construction work for the nation at war, the company is still regarded primarily as the constructor of many of the country's aerodromes, the remains of which are still clearly visible to the enthusiast and casual observer alike at a number of former sites. However, it is well worth considering its contribution to other military needs. Its important building and civil engineering contracts included the construction of a number of wireless stations, RAF training camps and equipment depots, and eleven barrage-balloon depots, on top of the staggering fifty-four aerodromes it completed under war contract, several of which were in Hampshire.

Arthur Witcher, speaking from his home in Canada, remembers his time in Hampshire:

Although war was declared, I think for some of us on the building programmes it was just 'carry on as usual', because we had already been involved in building for war, and now we were at war the enthusiasm on the gangs was far higher. I certainly never stopped to think about bombs and gas masks, and Germany invading us, I just was happy to contribute in my own small way to helping the war effort and to concentrating my efforts on giving our boys in blue the best sites to fly from and to. Whether I was helping to build a runway or a boiler house, the end objective was the same, to keep the RAF flying, and the flag flying proud for Britain, in time of war.

There was a considerable speeding-up in construction as a result of certain modifications and economies, and these were applied to three further contracts for permanent aerodromes that were awarded to Laing in the closing months of 1939. These aerodromes were among the first to include a concrete perimeter track.

Meanwhile, the company was also engaged in the building of three extensive camps for use as training centres by the RAF.

The development of heavier aircraft, and the course of the war during 1940, determined the need for considerable changes in the design and build of aerodromes. To meet the needs, efforts were directed to the construction of runways, dispersal areas and perimeter tracks rather than to site buildings, which by now were constructed as 'temporary'. Special runways for crash landings involved considerable civil engineering work, because at 3,000yd long and 250ft wide they were five times the width of the normal runway. On one site, for example, the work extended over an area of 600 acres, with 70 miles of drains and cable ducts installed and over 1 million cubic yards of excavation.

Interestingly, as the weight of bombers increased, further new methods of runway construction were introduced, using high-grade concrete of considerable strength. This required the use of 'scientifically prepared' sub-grade with sub-base and finished surfacing.

On permanent aerodromes, such as those at Stoney Cross and Ibsley in Hampshire, accommodation was built to a high standard, with well-furnished messes, sick quarters, married and single men's quarters in a style referred to as having 'a substantial and pleasing appearance'. Other buildings of substance included the watch office and control room, boiler house, parachute stores, dining rooms, technical buildings, workshops and stores and, of course, the hangars.

The following gives an idea of the main quantities of materials and the statistics of build in the construction of one of the permanent class of aerodrome, consisting

The control tower, always a welcome sight for returning aircrews. (*J. Laing*)

of a mix of both brick and concrete buildings. There would be 8 miles of roads, some 4 miles of water mains and 15 miles of drainage. To this, in terms of cost, would be added 7.75 million bricks, 850 tons of reinforcing rod, 17,000yd of vibrated concrete and 750,000ft of shuttering. On one construction site alone over 112 miles of scaffolding were in constant use day and night, with a workforce of 1,140 men engaged in shift work even through the bitterly cold winter months.

As economies and needs changed, so buildings became more austere in appearance and internal fittings and refinements had to be omitted. Speed of construction rather than quality of the buildings resulted in the erection of hundreds of semi-permanent and temporary buildings of every description, which, unlike the earlier permanent aerodrome layouts, were set on sites dispersed over a wide area as a precaution against enemy bombing.

Aerodrome construction was aided by the use of giant Koehring and Caterpillar tractors towing Scrapers, imported from America, which regraded vast areas of land in preparation for the construction of runways. These units were first used in Hampshire. Apart from these machines were fleets of lorries, sometimes supplemented with horses and carts when the need arose, trenching machines, concrete mixing plants, an on-site laboratory to test the quality of the concrete, spreading and compacting machines and machines for laying tarmac.

The challenge of building an aerodrome or a major supply depot was in essence equivalent to building a village, not least because all the main services needed to be provided. These would often include railway branch lines to connect to the main

Giant Koehring and Caterpillar units cleared land for airfield construction in Hampshire. (*J. Laing*)

rail network. The railway would enable stores of all types to be easily shipped to and from the sites, thus speeding up the vital supply line to the RAF on the Home Front, and subsequently on the front line. Trees had to be felled, streams diverted and telephone lines installed, and sewage treatment plants built when the local sewerage system could not be used to service the aerodrome.

In addition, the teams of men building the site had to be fed, watered and accommodated, and this in itself was a huge logistical challenge. Avril Day of Winchester remembers:

> Some of the chaps used to come to the house for a bath and a good home-cooked meal. Mum and Dad were good hosts and these men were really glad to meet our family and some of the neighbours. Some of the men had come over from Ireland and others were here from France, Pakistan and I think there was one Australian.
>
> One of the chaps, Brian, used to read my brother and me a story on the evenings he came down. I think he missed his own children very much and he adopted us in a funny sort of way. Once we went up to the airfield to visit the men, and although they were very busy they had time to say hello, and one of the foremen let us join them for a cup of tea during their break.

A runway under construction.
(J. Laing)

An Avro York of 246 Squadron at Holmsley South airfield. *(J. Laing)*

One day they all came down to the house to say goodbye because they had to go away on another job. Everyone was very upset that they were leaving and we often wondered what became of them. After the war, in about 1951, Brian, the chap who used to read us stories, paid us a surprise visit with his family. Sadly, his wife had been killed in a bombing when German planes had let go of their loads too soon and missed their target, which was a factory. His two children had survived and so had his widowed mum.

As early as 1940, when the British Expeditionary Force was evacuated from Dunkirk, and subsequent to the Battle of Britain, the wheels were set in motion for the eventual invasion of mainland Europe. The programme of building airfields continued to expand, and by 1942 an estimated 20,000 men were deployed solely on the construction of new sites. These airfields, particularly those in Hampshire and in the south of England, would be on the front line and would enable the RAF and Allied aircraft to undertake sorties ahead of and during the eventual invasion campaign.

Holmsley, for example, built at a contract cost of £588,042, was officially opened in October 1942, and during its four years as a commissioned station was a home base to units of RAF Transport Command, Coastal Command and the United States Army Air Force. A standard three-runway configuration, with dispersal sites and accommodation over a wide area, Holmsley had five of the T2 types of hangar as well as a number of temporary buildings.*

---

*   Flying from the aerodrome during the war years were a total of eleven squadrons with various aircraft including Mustang IIs, Spitfire 1XBs, Mosquito IIs and Typhoons.

Elsewhere, a conference held in the grounds of the Exbury estate near Southampton determined the practical logistics of maintaining supplies to an Allied army invading mainland Europe. This army would have to be landed at and supplied through beaches along the coast of northern France, where no safe port facilities existed. The Exbury conference determined that floating harbours would be the solution to what at first seemed like an insurmountable problem. And so the story goes that on a warm July afternoon, in the shade of a mulberry tree in the grounds of Exbury, the floating harbour was given what was to become its highly symbolic and emotive name.

The massive task – even by today's standards – of planning and constructing a prefabricated floating harbour twice the size of the harbour at Dover was undertaken from August 1943 to June 1944. The task involved the design and build of 6 miles of reinforced concrete caissons, 10 miles of floating bridging supported by hundreds of concrete and steel pontoons, and twenty-three pier heads. For its part, Laing constructed ten of the largest concrete caissons, known as Phoenix units, and forty of the floating pontoons, which were known as Whale units. Obviously, all those involved in the construction of the Mulberry Harbour, be they workmen, suppliers or company executives, were united in the challenge to complete the build as professionally and efficiently as possible. It is worthy of note that Laing, at the peak of the build schedule, was able to construct two units side by side in a record time of twenty-seven days, with the final fitting-out taking just a further seven days.

Field Marshal Bernard Montgomery paid a visit to one site to see for himself the work in progress and to impress upon the workforce the importance of what they were doing. Jack Stott remembers:

One of the huge structures built for the Mulberry project.
(J. Laing)

There was a buzz that went round the yard, and, before we knew it, Monty was walking along surrounded by officials and Army officers. I know I got a feeling of pride and excitement, because you knew if Monty was involved, we would achieve great things. He spoke to us in his familiar succinct way and he got a great round of hoorays and cheers as he finished his speech.

We knew what we were building was of great importance, and to have Monty tell us that in person was a tremendous boost to our spirits. None of us could have imagined the outcome of the work that we did. The war was something that changed everyone's lives. You cannot really explain it, but this country was totally united. Something we will never see again.

In October 1943, the women of the WVS began an emergency feeding programme for many of the teams employed on the construction of the Mulberry Harbour both in Southampton and at other sites on the Hampshire coast. They were told they must concentrate on their own work and see nothing of the work upon which the men were engaged. Because the men worked shifts, the WVS was called upon to provide round-the-clock catering, including breakfast, often in the open air under pouring rain.

On the morning of 6 June 1944, 10 miles of floating piers, 23 pier heads and 6 miles of reinforced concrete caissons were towed in sections across the 100 miles of the Channel for installation at Arromanches on the coast of Normandy. A number

of obsolete ships had already been sunk at Arromanches to form a preliminary harbour point. Only two caissons were lost as a result of mines, the rest being degaussed to protect them against the risk of magnetic mines.

The contribution of John Laing & Son to the war effort was encapsulated in the success of the Mulberry Harbour and the eventual liberation of Europe. Without the 'service beyond the call of duty' attitude adopted by Laing and the other principal contractors, it might be argued that the nation's capabilities in terms of defence and attack would have been seriously impaired.

Built in Hampshire, these sections formed part of the Mulberry Harbour, seen here in use off the coast of France. (*J. Laing*)

6

Defence of the Realm

It was so peaceful, and sometimes, despite the sight of military vehicles and people in uniform, it was difficult to believe there was a war.

(Doris Paice)

Local Defence Volunteers were ready for action. Ingenious positions known as 'stop lines' were introduced as part of the countrywide plan to create a strategy of defence in the event of invasion, and, supported by the WAAFs, the men of the RAF provided another line of defence in the skies.

Humour in wartime was one of the best defences against anguish, despair and shock, and the Local Defence Volunteers, later the Home Guard, provided great scope for the comedians in the community. Wally Penny recalls:

In the early days, before they became the Home Guard, they were the butt of many jokes. Everyone knows the nickname 'look, duck and vanish', but many of the nicknames they had were very rude. I won't repeat what was said.

Chris Lewis says:

My father was in the local Home Guard and I often went with them as they patrolled the local area, presumably looking for enemy paratroopers or shot-down aircrew. I can't remember them ever finding anything other than vast amounts of the metallic chaff known as 'window' that was dropped by aircraft to confuse ground radar. For some unknown reason, our larder contained lots of this chaff, still in thick wads, that had not broken up in the air as it was supposed to. I can't imagine what my father intended to do with it, but he did tend to hoard things that might come in useful one day. I know that we had numerous bombs dropped in the general area, but I think that death or injury from dropping lumps of chaff would have been more likely in our area.

Tom Watson saw the Home Guard in action, particularly when firing at low-flying enemy planes: 'They stood in place without flinching and shot off round after

A contingent of the Home Guard ready to fight to the last man. *(Sharon Cross, SHM)*

round at the Messerschmitts, which were flying low and machine-gunning everything in sight.'

All across the region preparations for possible invasion, either by sea or air, or both, were considered the priority. It was considered, for example, that the main threat to the Hampshire–Dorset border region was an enemy force landing on the south coast and using the Avon valley, along the route of the A338, as an axis of advance inland. Here, as elsewhere, stop lines were created through the emplacement of pillboxes, the creation of fortifications, preparations for the use of anti-tank rails and road blocks, and the training and equipping of the legendary 'underground Army'.

The objective of what was to be known, in this case, as the Ringwood stop line was to deny east–west movement and vice versa, and presumably the use of the A338. The two channels of the River Avon are between 45ft and 90ft in width, and in 1940 they would have presented quite an obstacle for an invading force. The fast-flowing water is deep, and there are irrigation channels with steep sides, and although bridges cross each channel they are quite narrow. However, a single-track railway ran north–south, just 600ft from the water mill at Breamore, and this line in itself would have been very easy for any light mechanised force to cross.

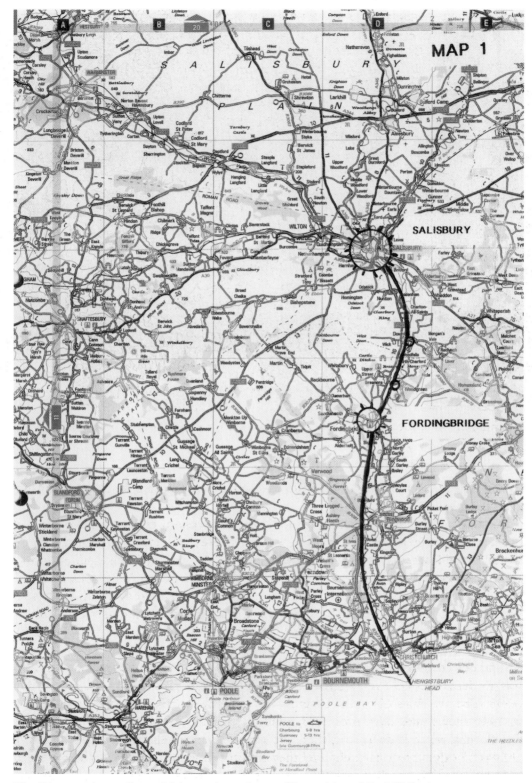

The Ringwood stop line, which cut through west Hampshire. *(Nigel Walker)*

The crossing point at Breamore, near Fordingbridge, was defended and fortified as part of a network of fortifications to cover both possibilities – attack from the west (the A338), and attack from the east. Part of the stop-line defence can still be seen today, and for those interested in how the county would have attempted the defence of the realm in the 1940s it is worth some study. Three pillboxes provided almost 360-degree coverage of the crossing point. The first pillbox, situated right on the bank of the river, is a modified Type 26 of concrete and brick, and it was emplaced to cover the Breamore–Woodgreen road from the west. Part of the blast wall was removed, possibly to enhance the field of fire from one embrasure. Faded red paint suggests that attempts were made to camouflage the structure, because it would have been a logical step to make it blend in with surrounding buildings, all of which are of natural brick. Effective fire from this emplacement and the exposed approach would make access by the enemy extremely hazardous. Pillbox two, also a Type 26, is on the north-east corner of Breamore Mill and was sited to cover the open area across the water meadows and the Breamore–Woodgreen road. However, the third emplacement is unique, having been built in part of the mill outbuilding. Unlike pillboxes one and two, this emplacement is extremely well camouflaged and is not immediately obvious to the passer-by. The position of the mill and pillboxes on what is a small island area between the channels of the river provided good observation and defence potential.

So, to the passer-by, there is no obvious indication of the former importance of the mill site. One's attention is drawn rather to the chocolate-box façade of the mill building and the rushing waters of the Avon. It is only upon much closer inspection that the gun slits become obvious. Fortunately, this stop line was never used in an invasion scenario and it is pure conjecture as to how effective it would have been in full operational service.

Bernard Job joined the Royal Air Force Volunteer Reserve in June 1942, following acceptance for aircrew duties. He was nineteen years of age.

At the initial Training Wing it was decided that I was suitable navigator material, and so I, with many others like me, embarked on the long training process, both in this country and in Canada. I was commissioned and finally gained my observer's brevet in September 1943.

I then joined the Operational Training Unit at Greenwood, Nova Scotia, where we flew in Mosquito aircraft for the first time. It was much more exciting than the navigation training Ansons that we had flown in up to then. We were also crewed up with our pilots, all of whom had been specially selected to fly this particular aircraft, the Mosquito. I was crewed with Flying Officer, later Flight Lieutenant, Jack Phillips of the Canadian Air Force. In time we flew back to England and did further and more exacting training at the Mosquito Operational Training Unit at High Ercall in Shropshire.

Later during the war Bernard was transferred to Hampshire. He recalls:

It was April 1944 that I travelled south and eventually stepped off the train at Hinton Admiral Halt, near Christchurch, where I was greeted by a WAAF driver. She was waiting to take me to Holmsley South, which would be my first operational station. Things were going to be rather different from then on!

Jack Phillips and I were members of 418 City of Edmonton Squadron, Royal Canadian Air Force. Almost all of the pilots were from Canada, other than the Squadron Commander, Wing Commander Tony Barker, who was career Royal Air Force. There was a fair sprinkling of RAF VR navigators too, and one Jamaican – Frank Smith was his name – among the crews.

Holmsley was in 11th Group of Fighter Command and, with a very few other squadrons, classified as a night intruder squadron. We had Mk VI Mosquitos, the fighter/bomber variant equipped with four 20mm cannon and four Browning machine guns. They could also carry two 500lb bombs when necessary. The

Bernard Job and Jack Phillips. *(B. Job)*

squadron's main task at that time was to surprise and intercept enemy aircraft over their airfields at night and – shall we say – generally to disrupt enemy airfield activity.

Ground targets were also attacked and, says Bernard,

Given the opportunity, we attacked ground targets. No airborne radar, known as AI [Aircraft Interception], was available at the time, but, despite this, the squadron had already achieved a creditable record of kills during operations over enemy territory, mainly at night. The usual pattern when ops were on was the night flying test in daylight hours to check serviceability and later, when targets or patrol areas had been allocated by group, flight planning and pre-flight briefing. Crews were given considerable flexibility in determining and routing to target areas – a privilege extended to very, very few other squadrons.

Navigation was still fairly basic. Bernard recalls:

Most operations were carried out at low level, little more than normal circuit height in fact. Good visibility was essential for the job, and so reasonable weather conditions were crucial. Navigation was decidedly basic, with an accurate flight plan followed by dead reckoning and the limited map reading possible using major landmarks, for example, rivers over the darkened continent, all of which really had to suffice. What was called the G Hyperbolic Navigation System was very new and only helpful to us within range nearer home.

From the front-line airfield near the Hampshire coast, Bernard was among the many crew who took part in missions ahead of D-Day.

Squadron morale under Wing Commander Barker was high, and after a few familiarisation flights we did our first patrol. Other operations followed, usually to enemy airfields in France. During this part of Operation Overlord, that is the build-up to D-Day, squadron aircraft were in action just before the landings to bomb airfields and cover some of the parachute drops that occurred.

Once the Allied landings in Normandy had been accomplished, 418 Squadron aircraft stepped up their operations in France in order to suppress German night-fighter activity against our bombers. The French airfields meantime had been considerably reinforced, and our aircraft often met intensive flak and persistent searchlight coning. The latter was sometimes countered by the decidedly dangerous tactic of diving down the beam and dousing the installation with cannon fire.

After D-Day, Bernard became familiar with the threat from enemy missiles:

Very soon a new threat appeared in the shape of the V1 missiles, which were very fast, pulse jet-propelled bombs, dubbed by us as doodlebugs or buzz bombs. They were, however, no laughing matter and were causing many civilian casualties in and around London and the south-east. So the squadron then took on the additional task of what were called anti-diver patrols over the English Channel at night. Diver was, incidentally, the military code name for the V1.

There were two kinds of operation involved. The first was direct attacks on any V1s seen. They had a very visible exhaust trail, so one could spot them fairly easily. Operation two was using spotter patrols to identify the launch sites in the Pas de Calais area so that bombers could be sent in later.

As you may know, downing the V1s in flight proved difficult when attempted at low level because at about 400mph they were able to outrun the Mk VI Mosquito, which did something like a maximum of 350mph at sea level. So it was that Squadron Leader Russ Bannock RCAF, who later became Wing Commander and Commanding Officer of the Squadron, and Squadron Leader Don MacFadyer evolved an attack strategy of patrolling at 10,000ft and diving steeply to intercept while accelerating to about 430mph. This meant that an interception proved highly successful and altogether the squadron shot down eighty V1s in the period until August 1944, when the launch sites were overrun by the advancing Allied armies.

On 13 July 1944, 418 left Holmsley South for nearby Hurn and then quite soon afterwards we went to Middle Wallop near Andover. But throughout all this the normal pattern of night intruding went on, sometimes deep into Germany, and the tally of aircraft kills increased with, luckily, relatively few losses ourselves. By the time 418 was transferred out of Fighter Command into Second Tactical Air Force in November 1944 the score sheet of No. 418 Squadron totalled some 178 aircraft destroyed, including 105 in the air. Thereafter, our operations were in support of the Allied armies on the ground, with rather more bombing sorties mostly at night and at low level.

A Laing-built guardroom of the type erected on permanent airfields. *(J. Laing)*

Looking back, the former 418 crew members remember some of the good times at Holmsley South, as well as the bad when things went sadly wrong – for example, when we made a count after a series of sorties and found we were missing friends who were not to be seen again. That was very upsetting, but we had to pull ourselves together and get on with what we had to do. There was no time for grieving.

Bernard has other memories of his time in Hampshire:

The Cat and Fiddle pub, which today is still a very popular meeting place on the main road between Lyndhurst and Christchurch, was a popular venue when crews had been stood down for the night. Occasional horse riding in the Forest was memorable – particularly for those like me who found it hard to stay in the saddle!

On the airfield the daytime flying discipline of rocket-equipped Typhoon Wing, also stationed there, was quite impressive. The occasional crash on take-off reminded us of the vulnerability of these Napier-engined aircraft. We were forever thankful that we had the incomparable Rolls-Royce Merlins in the Mosquito. Operationally, there were many times when plans went wrong and we had to extricate ourselves from trouble. On a daylight sortie to engage Luftwaffe aircraft on the Baltic coast, we had to abort when we were hit by intense anti-aircraft fire over the Danish coast. We limped home to base, thanks mainly to my pilot who was seriously wounded (I suffered only minor shrapnel wounds). We were together again on operations just three months later.

Another kind of experience was that we had one night over enemy-occupied Holland during a storm in which we encountered St Elmo's fire. With our navigation lights on and off and our props two circles of fire, we felt pretty exposed for a time. But we got through it and survived!

All in all the same team, Jack Phillips and I, completed forty-four sorties on 418 Squadron.

A former airfield building in the west of the county stands in silent testament. *(Author's collection)*

❖ ❖ ❖

In support of the Royal Air Force were the wonderful women of the WAAF. Doris Paice left the shores of England in 1948 for new adventures and a different way of life in New Zealand. Sharing her memories from the other side of the world, Doris looks back on the war years with mixed emotions.

I served in Coastal Command and initially I was based on the west coast of England, but then I was transferred to the station at RAF Calshot at the southern tip of Southampton Water in Hampshire, which was well known as a seaplane base. The flying-boat sheds I remember, of course, because they were huge, and today one of them remains as a well-known landmark. Calshot was also one of the main centres for the Air Sea Rescue Boats.

The Commanding Officer there was one of the old school, and I believe he was the Commodore of the RAF Yacht Squadron during peacetime. He was very interested in yachting anyway, and knew really everything about charts and so on. I was one of the chart girls, and my trade was Clerk/GD/Maps, responsible for correcting Admiralty charts from the publications that were being issued by the Admiralty to all Sunderland bases and Air Sea Rescue units.

The need to update charts on a daily basis was vital.

Oh, yes! You have to realise that with so much disruption everywhere the navigation channels for ships and so on were changing all the time. The Admiralty was putting out changes to the charts every week for simple things like changes to the lighting on buoys, shifting sands and the movement of lightships to identifying mined areas, and all the wrecks as well. Here of course the charts were used by the Air Sea Rescue lads and by the seaplanes and flying boats because their crews needed to know where it was OK to touch down, as well as to know if they were flying over 'safe' water.

The site at Calshot is very much part of the nation's military history. Doris continues:

This has a long history because of the old castle, which is right on the spit. Before the

The young Doris Paice. (D. Paice)

The engine from Calshot has been preserved and is now operated by the Tallylyn Light Railway in Wales. *(Tallylyn Railway)*

Second World War it was a peacetime base, and we WAAFs were billeted in what used to be the married quarters. We were allocated rooms which each accommodated three WAAFs, and it was very comfortable considering the age of the buildings and the fact that we were on an exposed promontory.

There was a small railway which ran the length of the spit, because the whole area was part of the establishment. At the western end there was the old officers' club, and at the eastern side was the main centre and the waterside activities. The train with its small wooden coaches was out of bounds for the airmen, but the WAAFs were allowed to use it to travel to the Chart Offices. Riding on the train was always a novelty, and just something different and something I think we all remembered as part of the experiences of the war we shared at Calshot.

Other memories come back to Doris of her time as one of the Commanding Officer's darlings:

I remember that the CO used to spend a lot of time in the chart room with the WAAFs, or the 'chart girls', as we were known. It was unusual for a senior officer to spend so much time with the other ranks, but he was always passing on his knowledge and he seemed to like the business of charting and navigation. We considered it something of a privilege that he wanted to pass on what he knew, but I think it was for this reason that we were not very popular on the base, because we were known as the Commanding Officer's darlings. We couldn't do anything wrong and we did lead rather a charmed life, as you might say. At the time I don't suppose we considered this anything other than normal, but looking back I suppose we did get out of a lot of the more routine jobs and things like drill. The work was interesting, and because it was shift work there were twenty of us to cover around the clock.

There was no public transport to speak of and cars were not available to us, so I used to cycle out around the New Forest whenever the opportunity occurred. I went up to Beaulieu and across to Lyndhurst, places I still remember to this day. It was so peaceful, and sometimes, despite the sight of military vehicles and people in uniform, it was difficult to believe there was a war.

I was posted to Chivenor in north Devon for a short time but went back to Calshot, and I was there when hostilities ended in Europe. I did move around with Coastal Command between my stints at Calshot, and was based in Stranraer, Blackpool, Carlisle and Turnberry. Needless to say, when the end came everybody went quite silly for a while and the relief was hard to describe. I know we had a huge bonfire at Calshot and part of the old train – well the wooden carriages – went on the fire. Some of the men burnt furniture as well. It was mad here, and I'm told that everybody was having a really good time in nearby Southampton too. Lots of people got really drunk, but who can blame them?

I had been in the Air Force for about five and a half years by the end. When I went home on leave I soon realised we were leading the good life in comparison with those in civvy street. I ate well and put on weight and we had good rations. I used to save up my cigarettes and sweets and take them home. We had chocolates in our rations and we did well, because the portions at home were meagre. I had sisters, and two were in the Land Army and one in the Army. My mother and father and elder sister all smoked heavily, so they had my cigarette rations.

There was never much in the shops, no meat, clothes, groceries and so on. They were hard times for the folk on the Home Front. When I was in the services I was in my own little world, as we all were on camp, and you really didn't have much of an idea as to what was going on around you. I served from 1941 to 1946, so quite a stint really, but it was very enjoyable and an experience that you cannot sufficiently describe to the younger generations.

I don't regret one day of my service and the small part I played in helping the war effort and the eventual outcome of good winning over evil.

7

The People's War

People were talking about gas attacks and wondering whether we would have gas dropped on us.

(Myrtle Smy)

Anecdotes from some of the many civilians and military personnel who experienced life in wartime Britain are a valuable testament to the country's heritage.

❖ ❖ ❖

Bob Bushell wrote:

Crews pose proudly with a De Havilland Mosquito: one of the finest aircraft of the Second World War. *(B. Bushell)*

I was posted as a trainee instrument repairer to number 125 Newfoundland Night Fighter Squadron at Hurn, and they were flying Mosquito aircraft at the time. My quarters were in a Nissen hut among a large area of rhododendron bushes on the other side, off the Parley-to-Christchurch road.

Because of the distance over to the dispersals area, we were issued with bikes, and these were to come in very handy on other occasions, such as visits down to Boscombe and Bournemouth. I occasionally attended performances at the Boscombe Empire of the model Jane of the *Daily Mirror* 'in the flesh' so to speak. A stage full of nudes, but they were standing like statues, as had to be the case in those days because of censorship.

In terms of aerial action, I managed to get a few kills before and after the Normandy campaign. In about August or September 1944, 125 was transferred to Middle Wallop airfield.

Mrs G. Walker remembers:

I was in the WAAF with an operational Mosquito squadron when they went to carry out the attack on the prison at Amiens. With the second front looming, we then went off in different directions, and I was sent to RAF Calshot. I was amazed at the change from busy squadron life to almost a rest-camp situation at Calshot. However, it was such a thrill travelling from the bottom camp to the spit head to

US soldiers under canvas in Hampshire, 1944. *(Author's collection)*

see the magnificent Sunderland Flying Boats gently rocking on the light waves in the Solent alongside the high-speed launches of the Rescue Service.

I loved the countryside around, and when I was duty driver I used to take baskets of carrier pigeons from the lofts to travel on the early train from Fawley station. We also went to the local pub in Fawley for evening drinks. That's us WAAFs, and the airmen from the base.

Occasionally, when we girls had days off, we went cycling over to Lyndhurst to have afternoon tea in a lovely little tea room. One of my little jobs was to go to collect the local padre from Blackfield to conduct the service at the camp on Sundays. When visiting Southampton on 'Swamps' [time off] as we called it, we saw many units of soldiers camped under trees almost the length of the journey.

Barbara Ashton (née Kemp), now living in New Jersey, remembers:

My father was the local policeman at Colbury, on the Lyndhurst road, and I remember one of his most unpleasant jobs was going out at night to finish off New Forest ponies that had strayed onto the road and been hit by cars during the blackout. They were able to wander all over in those days, and the car headlights didn't pick them out.

Every night about three o'clock we trudged across to the shelter at the big house over the road and I can remember searchlights lighting up the trees, and the hum of German planes overhead. Mum would always make us a cuppa when the all clear sounded.

One night a bomb dropped at the bottom of our garden. I remember the whistle as it came down. Fortunately I had asked my brother to get into my bed that night and it was just as well, because some shrapnel landed on his pillow where he would have been lying.

One Sunday morning something quite dramatic happened. The siren went and Mum called us from play seconds before a disabled German plane machine-gunned along the Lyndhurst road and across our lawn. People going to church had to jump into the ditches and it was lucky no one was killed or injured.

One unexploded bomb on Hunter's Hill, about half a mile away, went off when my brother was on the toilet and it blew him out into the hall. That was quite funny, I suppose, and you had to have a laugh whenever you could back then.

Dad came home one day with a parachute from a downed German plane and my aunt was able to make some lovely underwear and nighties for us all.

Many tank convoys came through on their way to the coast. One day my brother and I were riding our bikes home from playing in a local quarry, and I told my brother to get off his bike, which is what Mum had told us to do when the tanks were on the road. Soon after, a huge Churchill tank swerved and when I looked round I couldn't see my brother. Fortunately he had seen the tank coming and jumped from his bike and run into the woods. A good job too, because his bike was

Barbara Kemp is seen here with her brothers, all of whom served in the forces during the Second World War. (B. Ashton)

flattened. The tank crew were unaware of what had happened, but fortunately a dispatch rider saw me crying and stopped to help, as he had seen what had happened, and the flattened bike too. My mum had quite a shock when my brother went home on the back of his motorbike! We never got a new bike out of it.

Our biggest treat was when a NAAFI van overturned outside our house and we were able to help ourselves to Mars bars and other sweets that we rarely saw because of rationing.

Sometimes we used to stand outside and watch the dogfights over the area and the Ack-Ack guns shooting. When the magnesium plant at Marchwood was hit it burnt for three days, I remember.

We took the train to Brockenhurst for school, but it was delayed many times because of troop trains going through. We liked the Yanks best, because they threw out gum and chocolate for us. It broke up our hockey match on one occasion, as the train passed our playing field at Brockenhurst and we were showered with sweets thrown out by the soldiers.

My dad and the local men would sleep in the haystacks and hedgerows at night and were prepared to fight if we were invaded. I don't ever remember being afraid, and I give my parents credit for that.

Just before D-Day there were the Mulberry Harbour and landing craft in Southampton Water and all around Hythe.

Although we were not far from Stoney Cross, we never really saw the planes taking off and coming back. We did, however, meet a lot of the burnt airmen on the bus that we went to school on by then. The airmen were staying at Marchwood House, where they did pioneering surgery on burns victims. The men were encouraged to travel on the buses and meet people to help with their confidence. Although some were horribly burnt, I can remember Mum telling me not to stare. We did feel very sorry for them.

From South Africa, Alan J. Mclean writes:

I never forget our arrival, 31 and 34 Squadron South African Air Force attached to 205 Group RAF at Holmsley.

I asked the Flight Sergeant, who was in charge of servicing our Liberator, where the nearest town was. He said it was Christchurch and we asked how we could get there. Quick as anything, he said 'Harper's Taxi' and he gave us the phone number. When the taxi arrived it was a Ford 10 car and we could squeeze in only four people. There were eight of us, and when we asked the chap, he said he could not take us and return again for the other four because his petrol ration had run out. So I explained the situation to the Flight Sergeant and his response was 'No problem'. With that he came up with a jerry can of 100 octane aviation fuel and filled the tank of the Ford! Easy wasn't it? Mr Harper took us to a pub called the King's Arms, I remember.

A unique and fascinating shot of A.J. McLean, pilot, taken during an operational flight in a Liberator. *(A.J. McLean)*

At Holmsley – which was a very friendly place by the way – we enjoyed 5-star luxury compared to what we had been used to. In our smart Nissen hut we had real beds, proper mattresses, a stove for heating and some washing facilities in the same block. Marvellous and very happy times.

Life was always interesting, if not very scary at times, but one of the compensations was that as Air Force types we always attracted lovely girls to go out with. I was still very young so this was quite special really.

We flew mainly at night, so the day was spent preparing for this with briefings, sorting out kit, reading up and so on. One of the saddest memories I have is watching helplessly as my closest friend was shot down.

Betty Hockey, the founder member of the Non Stops concert party, recalls:

We were certainly not without risks visiting camps like the one at Bovington [Dorset]. They had a nice, well-equipped little theatre and we always enjoyed visiting this place. On one occasion, one of those really 'dark' black nights, our coach wound its way along the bleak country roads. We were a little late because of the slow progress we were making, and for that reason

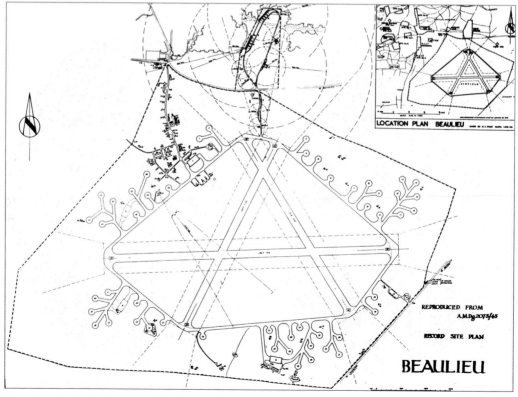

Beaulieu Airfield site plan. *(Author's collection)*

we all decided to change into our first costumes and apply our stage make-up in the coach.

Within a few minutes of our arrival the show opened without any loss of good grace from the audience. We were probably just a little over halfway through the show when the Red Alert was sounded. Usually, we would accompany the audience to the shelters and either chatter away or carry on as best we could with the show. However, this particular night our hosts thought it would be best if we got on the coach and drove away from the camp. This meant that the coach driver had to find the way off the camp as best he could without lights, and we eventually parked under some trees and waited for the 'all clear'.

We heard the impact of bombs dropping, not knowing where, but they seemed too close for comfort. It was frightening and we hoped and prayed that nobody would be killed or injured. A while later, we were able to return to the camp, but the theatre was not there. It had been hit during the air raid and we had had a very lucky escape.

One person who may have seen one of the shows by the Non Stops was Elsa Hastings, who was a member of the Women's Auxiliary Air Force.

I was Corporal 2053120 Goodhead E., a member of the WAAF. I served from 1941 to 1945, in the first days as a Flight Mechanic and later as a Fitter IIE posted to 102 Squadron Number 4 Group. For a time I was stationed at Beaulieu airfield

Elsa Hastings, née Goodhead.
(*E. Hastings*)

Elsa's post-war wedding to Ken Hastings.
(*E. Hastings*)

attached to the AFEE [Airborne Forces Experimental Establishment]. I had been posted before, but in the January the whole place in Lincolnshire was transferred out – planes, personnel, vehicles, if it could move or be moved, it went.

We arrived in Hampshire to find the whole area covered in deep snow, and on the airfield it was frozen solid. Regardless of rank or title, if we could not do our own work we were issued with shovels and put on detail to dig out a runway, as flying was crucial to our experiments.

Our accommodation was the next shock. The Nissen huts were bitterly cold and infested with earwigs, which dropped onto our beds at night. To try and save ourselves from these creatures we put cotton wool in our ears and elastic bands round the cuffs of our pyjamas – and the ankles too. Our sleep was often disturbed by the ponies, who rubbed themselves against the outside of the huts. They did that when they were itching, to try and relieve the discomfort. Instead they made us very uncomfortable!

Because of the frozen pipes, water had to be brought in by bowsers and this was used only for the kitchens and the camp sick bay. We had one metal bucket in our hut and we filled this with snow, which by the time it had thawed left a little water. This we used as best we could for flushing the toilet. We learnt to clean our teeth with snow, and the mixture of snow and toothpaste resulted in a mouthful of froth, which was difficult to get rid of!

When the eventual thaw set in we were gradually able to get on with the work we had been sent to do. As D-Day was drawing nearer, our Commanding Officer called all NCOs to a meeting. We were told that the planned invasion of Europe was imminent. Whoever was Duty Officer that night would be excused the rest of the meeting. It was me; I was Duty NCO! With the help of the Duty Officer, I spent almost the entire night rounding up some very merry WAAFs and sending some equally happy airmen back to their own quarters. Beaulieu was by then a very large station, and the accommodation was spread over a wide area.

The station was, of course, very active over the entire period of the D-Day campaign, but later things settled down quite a lot. I was released from the service in the August.

Myrtle Smy (née Lush) talks about the chatter on the school bus:

The boys and some of the girls used to take bits of shrapnel to school to show off what we had found after the raids. There was much discussion on Marvin's bus about the raids the night before and who saw what. What was hit, who saw the first dogfight, who saw a plane come down and how many German planes were shot down. One morning, in contrast, there was a lot of subdued talk about the local searchlight battery, which had been hit with loss of life

Myrtle also remembers:

One day a German bomber swooped really low down over the river and let a string of bombs go before pulling up over the trees and heading for home. The plane was so low that from the gardens we were clearly able to see the pilot. We had seen the enemy, a man flying his plane, like our chaps flew their aircraft over Germany.

Later, when there was a camp near our house, I used to watch the sergeant as he showed his men how to strip down a Bren gun and reassemble it. The cook there used to dish some of us helpings of pudding. The men used to sit outdoors and eat. When there was a raid or when officers arrived, we made ourselves scarce and flew off like rabbits through gaps in the hedge. We fetched and carried full and empty tea mugs to and from the cookhouse to the crew at the gun site. Then we were allowed to sit up on the gun and look through the sights and turn the handles, with help from one of the men, to swing the gun around or to raise and lower the barrel.

I was quite good at repairing socks, so the soldiers used to give me darning to do, but it took me a time to finish each pair. I was not that quick. Then I used to sketch pictures of girls from magazines and the soldiers tucked them into their wallets and off they went.

Born in 1923, Joyce Wilkinson (née Maton) of Thorney Hill had just turned sixteen when war was declared. Today she lives within a few miles of where she was born and where she experienced life on the Home Front.

My dad, Edward (always known as Ted), and mum, Irene, were country dwellers through and through. Dad was a builder so he had a responsible job in terms of war work and he had a reserved occupation. Later in the war he was working on the big airfield at Holmsley, and then went on to become clerk of works when the aerodrome had been completed.

Mum was a professional cook who worked locally, and obviously in wartime this proved invaluable, because she was able to make the best meals out of the rations we had as well as the produce we were able to get locally. There were always rabbits and chickens and eggs of course, so we were able to supplement our diets and really we ate well and we were healthy for that.

I was employed on a local farm doing a lot of the basic but very essential jobs. My work, too, was a reserved occupation, and we put in long days because there was always so much to do. I used to cycle to start work at about six o'clock in the morning, and although we were supposed to finish at four or five in the evening it was always much later than that in the summer months.

We used to have get-togethers in the Women's Institute hut at Thorney Hill. Funnily enough, it has only recently been demolished. We would have tea, but no coffee, of course, because we couldn't get any. We had soft drinks too, probably just lemonade, but I can't remember.

The work was hard but essential. Joyce remembers it fondly. *(J. Wilkinson)*

My family took in an evacuee for the duration of the war. We became friends, although she was younger than me, almost like a younger sister. Sadly, she died in a car accident some years after the war.

I met my husband-to-be, who was a cook with the Royal Air Force. It was my job to collect swill from some of the local military establishments, and it was while visiting one of these places that I first met Albert. Dad used to invite some service personnel to the house for a meal and a bath. That was something civilians used to organise for service people stationed nearby. Anyway, Albert was one of the chaps who used to come over to the house, so of course I recognised him and we began chatting, and that's how we became friends, and eventually husband and wife. After the war Albert was able to get a job as chef in a local youth hostel.

Myrtle Smy again:

People were talking about gas attacks and wondering whether we would have gas dropped on us. Nothing much seemed to happen in the early days after war was declared, but I often wondered, when I played in the local woods or field on my own, would I suddenly see German soldiers coming to fight us? If there was gas,

The young evacuee taken in by Joyce's family. The photograph was taken near one of the airfields in the New Forest. (*J. Wilkinson*)

how would I know, because no one would warn me? I thought too about coming home from school to find that my house had been bombed and I would have no mum. All these sorts of thoughts were going round in my head, but I was not scared, for all that. Later on, evacuees came to stay with us. They had lice and used to wet the bed.

My dad's job as an air-raid warden involved walking for miles around lanes and woodland paths, checking that the blackout blinds on the houses were closed up and not allowing light to show. He used to knock on doors to let people know he was about, and sometimes he used to come home laden with apples and bottles of home-made wine. So that his walkabouts could be sorted out into a route, the paths were named after London streets, with signs nailed onto the trees. I remember walking down Shaftesbury Avenue to Oxford Circus on many occasions! When the Army were camped there we never ventured into the woods because it was a bit scary, and I'm sure we were not supposed to go there anyway.

Len Lewis recalls:

Suddenly there seemed to be a lot of men and women in uniforms. Army, Navy, Air Force, there were nurses, more policemen and of course air-raid wardens. All the important local buildings began to be surrounded by sandbags, and there were soldiers standing guard with rifles. We soon got used to the barrage balloons hovering above us, but at first the sight of them was pretty scary.

Dad was in the Navy, and some time in the summer of 1940 he was invalided out because he was suffering from shell shock as a result of his ship being torpedoed. I remember seeing him walking up Bedford Street carrying a stool he had made out of raffia while he was having therapy at Haslar Hospital. Sailors were holding him under each arm and carrying his kit because he was still so unwell.

A few weeks later the first air raid took place while my mum, my brother and I were out shopping. We had to go into a shelter under one of the shops and we were given a helping hand by a policeman. He told Mum that he would keep an eye on my brother's pushchair, which we were not permitted to take into the shelter. When the raid was over, the policeman told my mum that a bomb had fallen on a pub that was not far from our house. We had to rush home because Dad was there alone and he was still very ill. We had not expected to be away

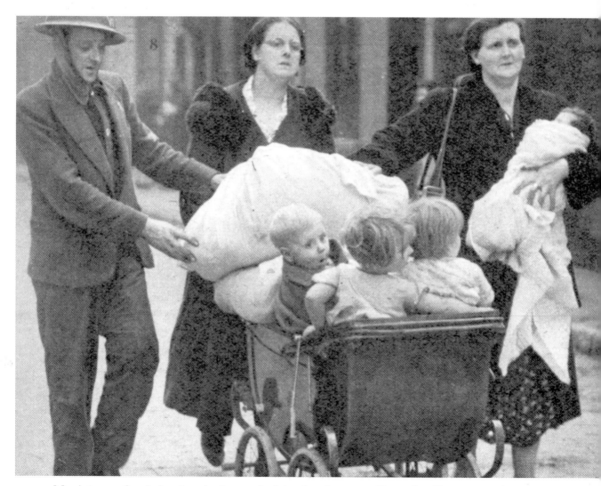

Moving on after being bombed out. A sight that became all too familiar across the country as well as in communities such as Southampton and Portsmouth. *(Private collection)*

from him for so long. I was quite frightened and confused by the way people were rushing about and talking quickly to each other. There were bells ringing all over the place, and fire engines and ambulances everywhere, and the injured people were being treated nearby.

John Clifford recalls:

My brother was in the ATC and I was in the JTC (now the Army Cadets). Some of the boys were in the Scouts and went on local camps. We went on route marches along the front to Boscombe and back, and had exciting times when a great column of cyclists went to Talbot Heath for a day's manoeuvres. We had only blanks for our rifles, of course, but putting a pencil down the barrel made a good substitute for bullets.

In 1944 the school returned to Portsmouth because it was considered safer now for civilians back in the city. So then my brother transferred over to Bournemouth School and I began work in the Prudential. I think I started at about £70 a year, but then a good lunch at Lyon's Corner House was only 1s 3d, and this was usually something like meat patty and vegetables, sponge pudding and custard and a cup of tea.

Betty Driver adds:

Apart from rationing and bombing and people getting on with their lives, all I can say is that, no matter how awful it was, England was like one big family and we all looked after each other. Even though we had rationing, we did manage to stay well and slim!

John Thornley wrote:

Looking back on my early life in those dark days, there were compensations as well as hardships. The continual need to make do and mend and the constant threat of death or destruction from German bombs were facts of life. We learnt not to complain and to be content with simple pleasures. Undoubtedly we were fitter and more thrifty because we had no chance to indulge ourselves. And because the adults were preoccupied with more important matters, we had freedom to play and developed naturally, which no modern child can hope to enjoy.

Len Lewis again:

One thing that sticks in my mind is the state of the sea and the beaches. There was a permanent smell of fuel and diesel oil as soon as you got near to the sea, and the beaches and water always seemed to be covered in debris, most likely

The young John
Thornley, seated in the
centre of this group.
(*J. Thornley*)

coming from sunken and damaged ships. Later in the war, when we could go
back onto the beaches, we always had to have a good scrub down when we
returned home from swimming in the sea.

Betty Hockey, the entertainer, recalls:

We must always remember those troops of the Forgotten Army. It was more than
a privilege to give those men a show. I was given a call early one morning with a
request whether we would go to Southampton Common that same evening. I
was told it was urgent, but I was given no details.

We arrived on time and there was an air of bustle, yet quiet calm and reverence. We were certainly not prepared for what we were to witness. Although pretty well shocked, there was no time for pity, the show had to go on and any questions could follow later.

These wonderful heroes had been brought straight off the boats at Southampton to the Intake Centre. All those poor men, feeble, weak, ill and starving. They were such a pitiful sight and so many of them missing front teeth that had been butted out by rifle blows of enemy guards. We were told to mingle and offer solace where we could, but were forbidden to even offer them a drink of water if they pleaded. Their condition was so bad that they had to be very slowly brought back to health by very strict dieting. I guess at that stage even their families did not know whether they were alive or dead. It must have been super for those families to be notified that they were indeed alive. I say alive – but only just. Some were too weak to sit on a chair and enjoy the show. Some merely lay passively on the floor, awaiting medical attention.

For them to receive kindness after so much torture and pain is beyond comprehension. But the gratefulness showed in their eyes far more than any words could portray.

With some, we just sat on the floor beside them and held their hands. There was little we could do and tears flowed between us. So many have often said since that for somebody to hold their hand was comfort in itself. They knew that their dreadful ordeal had ended and that they could now start looking towards the future. How many of them made it back to full health? Very few I fear. Yes, the Forgotten Army surely paid the price of freedom through sacrifice.

Pat Phillips, a former nurse, contributes:

Even when men came back from the PoW camps, some were in a poor way, and you knew that they did not have much life left in them. They were glad to be home, they took peace in that, and I think many of us found new strength in seeing the bravery of the men coming home and so we coped with all the heartache of the casualty rates we had seen on the Home Front.

Police and medical records list how many civilians on Britain's Home Front were killed or injured during the years from 1939 to 1945. At the height of the enemy bombing campaign on the nation's towns and cities, between 7 September 1940 and 31 December the same year, 22,000 people were killed and 28,000 injured, with over 54,000 slightly injured between September 1939 and December 1940.

The final total of casualties as at 9 May 1945 was 60,595 killed, 86,182 seriously injured and 150,833 slightly injured. The First Aid Posts, under the wing of the ARP scheme, were to treat more than 165,700 people.

8

They also Served

We all knew that something very big was being planned, although we all got on with what we had to do and prayed that the war would be over before too long.

(Doris Russell)

People contributed to the war effort in many ways from baking bread for the Army to entertaining the troops. These personal recollections reflect the fact that everyone had a contribution to make.

Doris Russell tells of helping the war effort from a tiny village. Doris was born in August 1922 to Hilda and John (Jack) Russell, who owned the village grocery and baker's shop in Redlynch on the Hampshire/Wiltshire border. An integral part of village life, the shop was a meeting place for local people as well as a source of provisions. Whatever went on, you could always find out about it there!

After spending her early learning years at Redlynch School, Doris went on to secondary education at the South Wiltshire School in nearby Salisbury. 'People did not travel so much because there were not so many cars. It was a bit of an adventure. Nowadays I go into the city without thinking about it.'

It was perhaps inevitable that when she left school Doris would join the family business. And so it was that, in 1938, she began her apprenticeship as a baker. 'I enjoyed learning to make the bread, all different types we made then,' said Doris, 'and I was also responsible for bread delivery to our customers. In years gone by so much was delivered to the home, like meat, bread, and of course groceries. It was very neighbourly and it was a good way of keeping in touch with everyone.'

When war came, Doris received her call-up papers. However, the Bakers' Union made representation to the authorities to have her excluded from call-up. The case was made that Doris was engaged in a reserved occupation because she helped to produce vital foodstuffs. For the duration of the war, Doris helped maintain the food supply in her community. Indeed, with the arrival of troops in the area, the demand for bread increased substantially and Doris was working flat out to ensure everyone received their allowances.

We got our supplies of flour from Joseph Rank in Southampton. We were given extra allowances when possible, to help us with the demand placed on us by the military.

I was too busy to be really aware of what was going on. Although there were troops in nearby Downton, and of course in many other parts of the area, we were, thankfully, not too affected by the war. Yes, we had one or two stray bombs and we were witnesses to the blitz on Southampton. We could see the lights in the sky, the fires burning, and we could hear the aircraft. I also remember the bombers going over on the way to Coventry. Well, we didn't know it at the time, though.

One of the better aspects of village life at the time was the traditional Saturday evening dance. Doris recalls that the Orchid Dance Band provided the music, and she goes on to say:

I think it was Charlie, our driver, who was one of the musicians, and his sister Sylvia also played. We had the dances at the St Birinus Hall, which is still there today up on the Ridgeway. There was no alcohol and we were more than happy with a few soft drinks. The fun of it was that servicemen by the truckload would turn up, and I can tell you there were many shenanigans those Saturdays. You could write a book just about that, you know!

In contrast to those rather colourful memories, Doris is keen to tell the intriguing story of the soldiers and the pigeons. As the war progressed, the Army commandeered the loft space of several properties in the village. They also effectively commandeered the pigeons that Doris's father had kept for many years. Three soldiers and a truck were specially allocated to the task of taking the pigeons to distant locations and then releasing them to fly back to the lofts. This was all done in secret on a daily basis, and the Russell family had to keep tight-lipped about the activities.

I know that the Army sent a dispatch rider from Longford, and I know that there was some communication system between the castle at Longford and the house. Dad had a pass to accompany the soldiers when they went into the loft to deal with the birds. When it got near to D-Day, I remember that the dispatch rider actually had to stay over with us. Talking of D-Day, I remember, as everyone does from that time, the American soldiers arriving locally. Well, they were actually over at Downton and it was in 1943. We all knew that something very big was being planned, although we all got on with what we had to do and prayed that the war would be over before too long.

Doris is saddened that post-war generations seem to have received a diluted version of the country's history during the Second World War: 'It is very important that the contribution made by the wartime generation is remembered always. It must never be forgotten.'

Bert Stannard travelled south to do military service when he was conscripted into the Army.

My father was employed on the railways and I had two brothers and a sister. My mum was a full-time housewife, and although women worked in the mills, it was widely considered that a woman's place was in the home.

I left school at fourteen and when I was a bit older I had a driving job. I was driving for some time, but it was now 1942 and, inevitably, conscription papers arrived one morning on the doormat. I was summoned to Keberoyd Mill at Sowery Bridge and found myself enlisted in the Royal Engineers. The six-week training programme was the first challenge, and for a brief time I was driving trucks that were based at the railway goods yard at Ripondon. Of course, when we drove out at night we had no lights on the vehicles, so the practice was to paint the rear axles white and shine a tiny light off them. That way the vehicle behind was supposed to be able to see you. So we had a lot of running around, all a bit boring really.

The six weeks passed and the company was posted to Longmoor in Hampshire. Longmoor was a well-established military base, best known for its vast railway network and its training centre for military engine drivers. Anyway, we arrived there, and our job was to load up the lorries with railway sleepers and move them from one end of the site to the other. I think they told us to do that just to keep us busy. Longmoor was also a transit camp, so it wasn't too long – about four or five weeks I suppose – before I and my mates were posted away. We were Number 1 Port Construction and Repair Unit RE, and we travelled to London to set up our HQ in the Institute of Civil Engineers Building.

My eldest brother, Jim, was in the RAF Regiment by now. Those were the people who guarded airfields and that sort of thing. Jack, the youngest brother, was a driver for the Royal Army Service Corps.

After the posting to London came to an end, Bert was moved back to Hampshire.

On 4 May 1943 we were on the move again, off to Millbrook near Southampton. The Territorial Army Barracks staff were given the task of finding accommodation for 500 men per company for three companies. We were billeted on Southampton Common and at Taunton School. I was stationed at The Mount, 467 Winchester Road, Southampton, the HQ for Number 2 Port Construction, and from there I used to travel to the Waterside area of Southampton, where my contribution was to the construction of the Mulberry Harbour.

From mid-1944 to the cessation of hostilities the following year, Bert was engaged in various tasks associated with keeping the might of the military machine

Bert was a member of a construction unit that contributed to the building of the Mulberry Harbour. *(J. Laing)*

operational twenty-four hours a day, seven days a week. Later he travelled to Europe and helped with clearing up the debris of war and the repatriation of equipment. His retirement years are being spent within a mile or so of the site where he was based and where he saw out most of his years of military service. In remembering his time during the war Bert said:

There was great friendship among the men. You had a job to do and you got on with it, despite the hardships that the wartime situation placed upon us and everyone else. You were doing your bit to help the country and to win the war. Great times in many respects, sad times when one lost friends or family.

Charles William Collier of New Milton helped to keep the Army on the move by feeding the troops.

By the late 1930s, I had gained considerable experience as a baker in my own right. I was by then married. As a maker and supplier of a basic foodstuff I was given reserved occupation status at the outbreak of war in 1939. However, I was keen to do my bit and I applied to become a fire-watcher. For reasons that were applicable at the time, but that today might seem rather trivial, the police threatened to prosecute me if I engaged in fire-watch duties. To be honest, I can't even remember what caused all the fuss anyway. So, for six nights a week I was a member of the LDV, later the Home Guard.

It was in the early days and the whole thing was very hit and miss. It's true that we had broom handles instead of rifles, and some of our activities were really rather amateur and almost slapstick. Things improved in time and rifles began to be issued. We also had machine guns and Brens, but none of that happened overnight.

I received my call-up papers – twice in fact – but because by now we were providing bread for the Army I was not able to leave my job. However, my third call-up came, and that was on 11 June 1942. I was sent a rail permit to Andover in Hampshire. From there I went out to the big camp at Barton Stacey. I got a lift with some other chaps on an Army lorry. Someone had said that he could get us a lift to save us walking, but when we were on the way a whip-round for the driver was forced upon us raw and somewhat naive recruits.

Because I was in catering, I moved about quite a bit to feed troops as they in turn moved from one location to another. It was supply and demand, I suppose, but I enjoyed going to different places. D-Day itself came and went, and almost everyone you spoke to, at least in the military, knew all this was going to happen because you knew the troops from all over the country were moving into the south of England and you could see the build-up of vehicles and stores. We just carried on regardless, because it was not the thing to talk carelessly or listen to rumours. Our turn eventually came to ship out, and about 270 chaps went down to Emsworth and loaded up a landing craft with all our equipment and provisions. It was 18 June, I remember, which was D-Day plus 12 by then. We took our trucks for the stores and to use as a base for setting up catering facilities in the field. Everything had to be done really on a make-do basis, and we had to use a lot of ingenuity to ensure the men were fed. We were part of the Royal Engineers Assault Squadron under General Hobart.

When we got to the other side, we saw all the devastation caused by years of war, of course, and many of the places that the RAF had bombed – particularly in the months leading up to D-Day. You bedded down where you could. Not too many buildings were left standing, but I remember on one occasion staying in a three-storey building somewhere in Holland. We were on the bottom floor and there were captured Quislings on the floors above. All rather bizarre really.

A couple of things stick in my mind from those times. There were some lorries carrying nitroglycerine and they exploded. It was an accident, but about thirty-eight men died as a result. I also saw dead British paratroopers in the minefields. Those sorts of things really shook you up, I can tell you. One of the best sights, though, was seeing the Typhoons flying overhead. That was very reassuring, and I think most of us realised by then that the Germans were on their last legs. A German soldier surrendered to me in fact, and like all of us, it was obvious he did not want to fight.

Charles, by pure fate, met his brother Jim while travelling through northern Europe. Happily Jim, like Charles, survived the war.

Charles was discharged on 15 May 1945 and returned to civilian life. In retirement on the south coast, he has retained a very philosophical view of the war and the small part he played. 'None of us knew then the importance of D-Day and the fact that generations after the event, people would still commemorate it. It's good that the efforts of all those involved, and especially those who perished, are not forgotten.'*

Betty Hockey helped to entertain the troops with a touring concert party. With all the shortages, travelling around the Southern Command area was difficult, as Betty explains.

Yes, we faced many problems along the way of course, with tyres for our vehicles being one of the most noticeable. We were literally running on canvas with very little rubber, which meant that in winter, with the ice and snow, we had to put chains on the wheels to stop us skidding. There were no heaters in the cars, so we would all jump out at the end of the journey onto somewhat numb legs. When the tyres got so bad that we had punctures both going out and coming home, I realised that if we were to continue entertaining, then

* In the Hampshire town of New Milton, 'Dorothy's' café has served customers for seventy years and was a favourite haunt of many of the thousands of service personnel who were stationed in the area during the war. Charles is a member of the family that has owned the business and continues to provide sustenance to locals and weary travellers alike.

something pretty drastic must be done. The controlling of tyres in those days was done at Bristol, so off I set to confront the people there with our desperate position.

Surprisingly enough, they were very sympathetic and within a couple of weeks a set of tyres was delivered for each car. We couldn't believe our luck! Prior to our receiving the 'new' tyres the AA service was excellent, and they would ring me each day to know the route we would be taking. Somewhere along that route they would be waiting and without a word they would open the boots of our cars, take off the offending tyre and put on the spare wheel.

When we arrived at the camps there would be soldiers ready and waiting to take the punctured tyre and mend it while we were doing the show, and we would then set off for home with fingers well and truly crossed. We certainly could not have managed without those wonderful AA men, who still kept their eyes open for us even though we had new tyres fitted.

Another big source of worry was petrol. Although each car had an allocation, needless to say it was not sufficient. The camps and units were very good and helped us out as much as they were able, but because we were doing an average of five shows per week, the petrol did not stretch to that. Now and again people would give us a few coupons, which helped, but they were still not enough, unfortunately. Apart from our own private rations the Army gave us a small allocation, but as time went by and the demand on the concert party grew, I decided to apply to Reading, which was the regional control for fuel supplies. The end result produced two gallons more per car, which was not a lot, but at least enough to get us by.

We travelled in a convoy of three cars and a big Canadian staff car that was used for towing a trailer full of props and scenery. Looking back, it must have been a strange sight to passers-by and other road users. I well remember we were going to do a show for the Canadians on the cliff top at Highcliffe-on-Sea.

We chose the route just past the Cat and Fiddle at Hinton, and then we had to turn right into a very narrow lane. This was fine, except that all along the main road all four cars had been dodging in and out of an Army convoy of trucks and tanks, led by men in a Jeep. I was driving the lead car – complete with trailer of course – and to get in front of the convoy I squeezed in behind the Jeep. At the junction I peeled off right, into the narrow lane and lo and behold, would you believe it, the entire convoy followed me!

It was chaos. We were already late in getting to the unit and now we had to wait while every tank, truck and van was slowly backed up into the main road. It was truly hilarious. Afterwards we had a jolly good laugh at the confusion it had caused. I think one could liken it to the silent film days and the Keystone Cops.

I was the 'naughty one' doing the can-can, seven veils and the fan dance. All pretty much frowned upon in those days. Each veil would be thrown out to the audience, never to be seen again. My fan gradually lost its feathers, and ostrich feathers were absolutely impossible to obtain, so the act had to be dropped eventually.

On one occasion a unit of the RAF stationed at Beaulieu gave us a whole parachute. There were literally yards and yards of pure silk, but unfortunately, being silk, it would not dye. However, by immersing a few pieces at a time in strong dye and steeping them for days on end, we did produce pleasing pastel shades. We were able to kit the girls out in lovely long evening dresses, and the men with nice shirts. I also had another lovely costume for my Eastern dance.

We received much help from the police, which was Bournemouth's own police force in those days. They would make sure we had clear access around the area. After I had dropped everybody off at their homes I had rather a nasty, eerie lane down which to go to park the vehicle. It was quite safe in those days, but very eerie nevertheless. It was reassuring to know that there was always 'the bobby on the beat' nearby, who would see me safely home. That was a great comfort.

One night, around two o'clock, I was on my way back and was crossing the square, when out strode a policemen holding out his hand for me to stop. He commandeered the car and told me to drive to the cliff top as there appeared to be a suspicious character there. Sure enough, there was a man deeply entangled in the barbed wire that stretched all along the coast. We waited for the Black Maria to arrive and then I returned the policeman to his beat. Although very tired and wanting to get home, I found it very exciting and felt as if I had helped defend our shores, although I never knew the outcome of the night's events.

On another occasion our ventriloquist was walking home with his suitcase of dummies. He was challenged by the police as to what he had in the case. For simple devilment he replied 'Bodies'. He was immediately whisked off to the station. Fortunately, they saw the funny side of the situation.

Another night, to get to the Nine Yews Camp we hired a coach that the driver parked among the trees. The show went well, but when leaving the camp the driver caught the wing of the coach on a tree. He was naturally very concerned as to what his boss would say about the damage, especially as it was a problem getting spare parts. As usual, the Army came to the rescue and they soon had the wing repaired. Such was the way of the world in those days, everybody helped each other. Were we not all pulling to the same goal?

One evening we were doing a show for troops under canvas on the Lyndhurst-to-Beaulieu road, and to our surprise we found a soldier sitting at a sewing machine, busy treadling away. The material being used was a vivid yellow and very shiny. It was, I believe, the first of the Day-Glo material. He was stitching shoulder covers that could be seen at night. Needless to say, we returned home with a couple of bales that were used to fit out yet another show.

We had four different shows on the road, and I know for a fact that we were considered the largest, the best-dressed, the cleanest – yet on the borderline – and most popular concert party around the Southern Command area. Helping to keep morale high and some laughter in their lives, we had performed over a thousand shows by D-Day.

9

The Green Army

The WVS would appear from nowhere and set up a canteen and an information post for those who had been bombed out or who were coming to look for loved ones.

(Christine Lock)

Tea, buns, a listening ear and a lot more besides. The dedicated service of hundreds of thousands of women became synonymous with the essence of life on the Home Front and the spirit that helped to win the war.

When it became apparent to the enlightened few in Government that there was to be a war in the 'foreseeable future', the then Home Secretary, Sir Samuel Hoare, already deeply involved with the business of Air Raid Precautions, perceived a need for women volunteers to assist with associated work. Given the fact that the British were reluctant to consider such an unpleasant situation as war, and the possibility of air attacks on the country was not making enough people sit up and take notice, Hoare wanted to recruit a force of women to help achieve one million volunteers who would be put 'on standby'.

So it was that in 1938 Hoare approached the Dowager Marchioness of Reading, who was well known for her considerable experience in charity work. After first making a number of urgent telephone calls, Hoare contacted Lady Reading at her London home. He had discovered that, for one reason or another, either political or practical, existing women's organisations were not suitable as recruiting agents for a new force of women volunteers to assist the ARP.

His question to Lady Reading was: 'Do you think you could start something special?' Lady Reading, in reply, questioned whether she was the right person for the job, but she was assured by the Home Secretary that, at the very least, he wanted her advice.

A couple of days after her conversation with Hoare, Lady Reading went away on holiday, and during this time she produced a memorandum in which she set out suggested terms and guidelines for a new service to meet the challenges thrust upon it by a war. The document recommended that the Home Office should provide office space and some financial assistance for clerical work and for training fairly soon after enrolment. She believed that setting up the organisation in such a manner that all the women volunteers felt that it 'belonged to them' was paramount. She was only too well aware that the established practice in some organisations was to utilise snobbery and patronage to secure the desired results, and she could not envisage this being of any benefit to the new service.

The aims of the organisation were grouped under five main headings that addressed the purpose and remits of the already established ARP, and reflected its activities. Clearly, by tasking the organisation with enrolling women into the ARP service, up to mobilisation strength, the new service would bring home to all women, especially housewives, what air raids meant, and what the women could do for their families and for themselves.

The country was to be divided into a number of regions, each with a Regional Officer who would be responsible for getting in touch with all local authorities preparing ARP schemes. Women recruits would be responsible to the local authorities and would be given training and necessary exercises by each authority. Successful completion of the various training courses would be recognised by certification, and proficiency would merit a 'distinctive sign', such as a scarf.

It is interesting to note that during the consultation and fact-finding exercise for the new service, information was sought from foreign embassies in London about the role of women in other countries. Much was learnt from Spain about the work done by women during the Civil War, and the Russian Embassy advised the enquirers that women did the same work as men in the Soviet Union.

After some deliberation it was decided that the new service would be called the Women's Voluntary Service (for ARP), and the name was launched on 18 June 1938. Although they were allowed to enlist as ARP Wardens, it was felt that women did not have the physical endurance to sustain the required level of operation during heavy raid conditions! The role of women in the ARP was therefore

WVS regional office. *(WRVS)*

restricted to that of 'trainers', with the task of emphasising the need for basic ARP skills and personal training of women in the home. They were also recruited as ambulance drivers and assistants, and many joined the newly formed Transport Department as convoy drivers.

By the time war was declared, some nineteen different jobs were available to WVS volunteers, and training was extensive, over 800 courses being arranged in London alone.

The Ministry of Health had already requested information from the WVS as to how many bottles of water and milk and how many WVS escorts would be needed to evacuate cities such as London. When the agreed twenty-four hours' notice was actually given for evacuation, twelve telegrams were sent from HQ to Regional Administrators who contacted county and borough organisers, and they in turn made contact with centre, district and village representatives throughout the county. By using this simple yet effective protocol across Britain, some 120,000 women were alerted, and, of these, 17,000 acted as escorts on the first evacuation.

It is true to say that, through no fault of the WVS, actual numbers of evacuees allocated to specific areas were either under quota or far in excess of the numbers expected, and billets prepared for expectant mothers, for example, were often taken by schoolchildren, and vice versa. Given the vast exercise of moving people around the country, it is not surprising that in the planning process a few mistakes were made, but they were quickly resolved by the resourcefulness of the members of the local WVS, who were in a class of their own when it came to improvisation.

Once in situ, evacuees had to be provided with clothing, health care, social welfare and other support, all of which the women of the WVS attended to without so much as a blink of the eye. Local centres were to become clothing depots, medical centres, billeting offices and information bureaux, with members adapting as the challenges arose. Every aspect of day-to-day life was built on the solid platform of the local WVS centre and its willing members. They provided lending libraries, social events, receiving nurseries, furniture and repairs, toys for the children and communal feeding centres.

Later, their services became available to the men and women of the armed forces through the provision of a NAAFI-style facility that used both stationary and mobile canteens to provide a spread of hot and cold food, as well as chocolate, razors, cosmetics for members of the ATS, WAAF and Wrens, and the biggest single item of all, cigarettes. An average of over five million cigarettes was distributed every month via WVS canteens and hostels.

The canteen facility was also used very effectively as part of a plan to meet the psychological needs of the evacuated population. In an act of what can only be described as true understanding of people and humanity, the WVS responded quickly to problems experienced by evacuees, host families and visiting parents. Evacuation gave rise to many previously unforeseen challenges, and immediate action was needed both to meet them and to create as close to a 'normal' and stable home life as possible.

However, one aspect of evacuation became a serious irritant to host families. While most hosts were happy to welcome visits from the parents of evacuated

The WVS could always be relied upon to provide a meal. (WRVS)

children, they became quite alarmed by some parents who would arrive on the doorstep expecting to be fed, accommodated and entertained for the day or weekend at the expense of the host.

There was also the extra burden of becoming involved in family disputes, and typically these would arise either from the pleas of the children to be taken home, or from the evacuees' forthrightness in telling their parents that they never wanted to go home because life was better where they were. The latter was usually true in cases where children had come from abusive or very poor families and realised the benefits of building a new life with their host parents, many of whom, incidentally, were asking whether permanent fostering was possible.

And so the idea of opening a canteen for the use of parents and evacuees during weekend visits proved an immediate success. Not only was the canteen regarded as neutral ground, away from the home of the host family, but it was also a good place

Canteens were opened for parents to meet their evacuated children. *(J. Laing)*

for visiting parents to meet and talk to WVS and other agency representatives about problems, and to request help with various domestic and personal issues. Canteens also took away from host families the responsibility of entertaining and feeding the few thoughtless parents who always expected everything free.

People from almost every social and environmental background were thrown together and provided with accommodation either in a hostel or with families who were living in the 'safe' areas of the country and who enjoyed a different way of life. A child from an inner-city slum, for example, might be taken in by a farming family. This would prove to be either a delight to the child or so boring that the youngster might want to take to his heels and flee at the first opportunity.

The authorities responsible for evacuation had not fully realised that there was a fundamental difference between the outlook and lifestyle of people who came from poor districts of evacuated towns and cities such as Portsmouth and Southampton, and those of the average country householders. Much improvisation was called for at the beginning of the evacuation scheme, and this led to considerable problems, many of which landed in the laps of various WVS groups.

The WVS, within its widening remit, provided help, guidance and assistance to everyone who needed it. Pat Rouse recalls:

I was told by my mum that the WVS helped to clothe us when we were bombed out and that they organised new accommodation and contacted family members in Hampshire who later took us to safety in the country. I also apparently had a couple of small toys given by the WVS, and my brother was given a cricket bat.

Mum had to organise the change of address for ration books and ID cards and notify various people about our move, and the WVS helped with that too. I am sure if it hadn't been for them, our family and many other bombed-out families would have had real problems.

When, in the winter months of 1939 and early 1940, the expected raids did not happen, more and more women returned home with their evacuated children. Within just four months some 80 per cent of the mothers had gone home, taking with them 86 per cent of the children under school age. However, the older children, particularly those attending secondary schools, had settled better, and of these about 50 per cent remained as evacuees.

In the spring of 1940, the WVS Rest Centres were just being cleared of British and French soldiers evacuated from Dunkirk when a demand was placed upon them to look after evacuees from the Channel Islands, over twelve thousand Gibraltarians, and refugees from France and Holland. Later, as more refugees arrived from other parts of Europe, the WVS was called upon to provide interpreters and people with specialist knowledge of the refugees' countries of origin at ports including Southampton.

The German attacks on Belgium and Holland and the collapse of the Allied army in Europe necessitated the re-evacuation of some English towns and cities, and this too had a major impact on the WVS.

It was also in the spring of 1940 that the WVS conceived the idea of a messenger service, to be activated in the event of invasion, when phone lines and road links would have been cut by enemy forces. What began as the village bicycle shuttle messenger service in a small south-coast community was to evolve as the officially recognised Civil Defence Messenger Service.

The arrest and internment of aliens living in the country were now under way, and although it was the responsibility of the police to carry out this duty, members of the WVS were asked to accompany them on occasions when female aliens were being arrested and escorted to places of internment.

The WVS was also called upon to provide such comforts as books and food for the small children of internees, milk for babies, and assistance with writing letters to loved ones.

When the Local Defence Volunteers were being formed, they had very little equipment. Local resources, including the WVS, were called upon to assist. Brassards, first-aid kits, haversacks and camouflaged sniper suits were among the items made by members, some of whom were later engaged on special-purpose work, that of making Molotov cocktails for the use of the LDV.

But it was the making of tea that perhaps became synonymous with the WVS, because tea and a listening ear were all that many of those who came into contact with the service expected. Help beyond that was welcome, but the extent to which help was given surprised everyone. Christine Lock said:

> My granddad George was with the ARP, and often during his shifts he would be on the go non-stop, especially after a raid. He said that from quite early on in the war, as if by magic, the WVS would appear from nowhere and set up a canteen and an information post for those who had been bombed out or who were coming to look for loved ones. He said more than once that it was a strong cup of tea and a smile from the ladies of the WVS that lifted his spirits and gave him the energy to carry on.

Mobile canteens and kitchens became the cornerstone of the service's provision to troops, civil defence workers, those engaged in war work out in the countryside where no suitable facilities were available, and to civilians, be they evacuees or bombed-out families. In fact, anyone on the move in the country would have come into contact with a WVS mobile catering facility. They were everywhere, and in a short time the organisation had graduated from requisitioned vehicles to its own purpose-built vehicles, a number of which were donated by benefactors from home and overseas.

During this period too, the Housewives' Service of the WVS was enrolling members in large numbers in many towns. These volunteers undertook equally valuable tasks, including helping with salvage drives, rendering first aid where necessary, helping residents to clear up or salvage belongings, running errands of mercy, providing the use of baths and sweeping up broken glass from roads and paths. Inevitably, duties included making a 'nice cup of tea'.

A welcome 'cuppa' from a WVS mobile canteen. *(WRVS)*

Within a year of the declaration of war the WVS had also established itself, and rightfully so, as the organisation to which every serviceman and woman could turn for help, and this would be given to the limits of what was possible. Notwithstanding the demands placed on the organisation by civilians and by changing Government needs, the typical expectations of the service are summed up by an extract from one WVS area report:

Tea at an hour's notice for any number of people between forty and four hundred has become commonplace. Baths, laundry, salads, knitting of pullovers and socks for men, altar flowers for chaplains, decorations for the Mess, upholstery of chairs and sofas, provision of furniture on a hire purchase scheme, cakes and sandwiches for Concert Parties, billets for wives and children, constant supervision of the welfare of Anti Aircraft sites.

It was concluded that, whenever there was a job of any kind that was nobody's particular responsibility, it was handed to the women of the WVS, and it was always done.

The incredibly long list of jobs undertaken by the WVS also included changing library books for hospital patients; helping with national savings campaigns, including Warships Week and Salute the Soldier; making children's toys from recovered wood; finding furnished rooms; organising salvage drives; helping children's homes every morning and afternoon by taking the youngsters for walks; making blackout blinds; and acting as a registry for queries on housing, tax and many other issues. They located and prepared and cleaned homes for evacuees and others in need, organised basic furniture items, and even placed flowers in vases as a welcome gesture.

So too they organised what was to become known as the Pie Scheme, a catering service that delivered pre-cooked pies to workers on farms and in the countryside, to service personnel stationed in remote outposts, and to schoolchildren in villages.

When the United States began to send troops to Britain, the WVS evolved the idea of British Welcome Clubs, where GIs could meet young people of the neighbourhood. Over 200 such clubs were eventually established, and these contributed in no small way to acclimatising the population and the incoming Americans to each other's way of life.

And all this was done by volunteers, almost all of whom covered all their own expenses. Moreover, WVS members made enough time to contribute sufficient money to buy three fighter aircraft for the Royal Air Force. Robert Read recalls:

I was involved in one of the big building contracts near Portsmouth in readiness for the Normandy campaign. These girls used to come out in all weather, through rain, mud and very cold weather to serve us with food and drink. Whatever the day chucked at them, they always managed a smile and a few kind words.

One time a lass called Jane just accidentally slipped in the mud and went over. I am afraid she showed a bit too much leg on that occasion, and although

Impromptu wartime feeding, one of the vital services provided by the WVS. *(WRVS)*

thankfully she was not hurt, her pride was dented. After that we used to call her our *Daily Mirror* girl after the pin-up 'Jane' who appeared in the paper.

As the build-up to D-Day progressed apace, it was to the WVS that the authorities turned for assistance in packing equipment for the fighting men. Thousands of spare parts were packed in cartons, each containing from 5 to 200 items, and ultimately some 80,000 cartons were completed.

One cannot make mention of the WVS without including one unique aspect of the service that, with little recognition from the wider public, made a significant contribution to the war effort. The COGS scheme involved children in the task of collecting salvage, and to make the task more interesting a badge was awarded to the keenest young collectors. The scheme, which had the support of parents and the educational authorities, was to award a total of 192,523 badges, although it was recognised that many more than that number were earned during the period when the scheme was operational. The children had their own song and 'as little cogs in a big wheel' they made a tangible and much-needed contribution not only to the war effort, but also to the breadth of services offered by the Women's Voluntary Service.

Throughout the dark, traumatic and eventful days of the Second World War and the post-war repatriation of PoWs and the homecoming of the nation's servicemen and women, in the streets, lanes, cities and villages of Hampshire and across the country, the one million volunteers of the Women's Voluntary Service could be found involved in every aspect of daily life, helping everyone without exception, whatever their needs.

This poignant photograph of Zina Honeybell and Lorna Milligan, two COGS volunteers, is very evocative of the days of the war. *(WRVS)*

In the rebuilding of Britain and in the resettlement of its population, they went about their business without fuss or favour and displayed extraordinary courage, selflessness and determination for the good of all those whom they served.

10

On the Land, in the Air

It was an utterly unique and memorable experience and changed my outlook on life, and my life itself.

(Noreen Cooper)

A young woman worked on the land while a young man of the same age joined the RAF and was later to become a PoW. Here we can glimpse the contrasting lives of two teenagers at war.

Noreen Cooper left her native England to start a new life in Australia just four years after the end of the war. From there she tells the story of her experiences of the Home Front.

I was born in 1923 to William and Cecilia Bolt of Bournemouth. Dad was a Chief Petty Officer in the Royal Navy. I was to have two younger siblings, Gerald and Joseph. Bournemouth was in the county of Hampshire at that time. It was very much the famous seaside town that it is today. My earliest family memory is having tea at a place called Whale Island, part of the Portsmouth naval base. I remember seeing the old ships' figureheads on the lawns.

As you have probably worked out for yourself, I was sixteen years of age when the war began. I was living in Christchurch and had a job at Marks & Spencer. I was a trainee window dresser, and in those days the displays were always very grand, big and bold. I enjoyed the work. By the time war was declared, however, I had enlisted as a part-time messenger with the ARP service, but I kept my job at the store.

Noreen's life was about to change, as did the lives of many young people at the time.

A short time later I underwent two months' training at an agricultural college near Winchester in preparation for joining the Women's Land Army (WLA). That was OK, except the work we did was with poultry. I didn't like that at all.

When the training was over, off we went to put what we had learnt into practice. To begin with I had knock-backs from farmers who were not prepared to take on a seventeen-year-old. However, when I eventually managed to get a place on a farm it was a case of learning almost everything all over again, because they each had their own ways of doing things to suit the particular farm and it also depended on whether the farm had cattle.

On the farm where I was working, apart from milking we had to do thistle cutting, potato picking and hoeing, among many other important jobs. Harvesting started in June and went right through to October. We did the hay, then barley, oats, wheat and rye. It was really very, very busy and we had a lot of overtime, often working through till ten at night.

In the winter the thresher came and there was about a week's work on that. That was probably one of the worst jobs I had, especially when we were threshing clover seed. We used to get dirt money for that, an extra 2s 6d. We ended up looking like chimney sweeps after that job! We also used to pick peas, and we were given an extra 6d as an incentive to pick more peas. It worked, and we always delivered many more full sacks at the end of the shift.

One farmer we worked for during hay making used to keep us supplied with home-made cider. He used to say the more we drank, the better we worked. I'm not sure that's true, but he must have been pleased with what we did anyway. After drinking cider we used to go back to the billet and sleep through the air raids targeted on nearby towns. I suppose the drink did have a positive effect on us in that respect.

By the way, I was taken off milking duties because I contracted dermatitis from one of the harsh dairy cleaning products.

Noreen remembers her time farming with great enthusiasm:

Most of the time it was fine – hard work, but fine all the same. And there were new experiences every day. Yes, there was bound to be some routine, but you met so many new people who, like you, were doing their bit for the country and who always found reason to laugh and joke. That was such a good tonic, the ability to see the funny side of everything.

The farm at Lower Ashfield, for example, was right on the main road. There were troops camped all around and seldom a day went by when we didn't have an audience. At times it was embarrassing, but then they used to help us if they could, especially at harvest time. Of course, there were the usual remarks and high jinks, but so what, in those days you grabbed life and made the most of it. Tomorrow you could be dead.

I clearly remember hearing pipes and bugles being played by the soldiers on cold frosty nights. It still sends a shiver down my spine to think about it now.

Inevitably there was at least one job that no one enjoyed:

Noreen Cooper enjoyed
her wartime experiences
in the Land Army.
(N. Cooper)

Definitely, it was having to cut the kale, and also picking the sprouts in winter. They were either wet or full of frost and you would end up thoroughly wet through, and of course you had to stay in the same wet clothes all day. It's no surprise that so many of us ended up with arthritis and bad backs. Another job that none of us liked was sorting potatoes from a clamp that had not been opened for months. Lots of them had rotted and you might accidentally pick one up, all slimy and rotten, and the smell was terrible.

Mind you, the good ones we used to roast, and sometimes we would clean a shovel to toast our sandwiches in the fire. We had an allowance of 12oz cheese per week, so our sandwiches were always cheese!

Working in the countryside meant that there were relatively few alarms.

Well, of course the sirens used to go off locally when attacks were about to happen on some of the nearby towns, although sometimes we did not hear them. At one site we had a man on a bike who came round blowing a whistle. Often it was too late to get to safety, so we used to hide in the hedges or under one of the tractors. At another place we didn't need to hear the sirens, the pheasants began shrieking!

Noreen was quite charmed when she met prisoners of war, and recalls:

They were Italians, and they were dropped off from a truck which went round to a number of farms on the first day, allocating various prisoners. They were unshaven and really a sad and sorry lot of men. But after realising they were working with girls on the farm, they arrived next day all smartened up. One chap wore a flower behind his ear and a fancy, lady's scarf around his neck. He was always happy and singing – I think like all of them he was glad to be out of the war.

The prisoners would receive food parcels from home and these all came in aluminium containers. The men would make rings out of them, and I still have an engraved cigarette case made from part of a container. Later the men were allowed out of their camps to go into town. They proved to be very trustworthy and generally they were very friendly and happy people.

By the way, for a while we worked with a conscientious objector and I do feel ashamed to this day about the way we treated him. But in those situations I suppose we reacted in the way we did because we were all supposed to be helping to win the war, for his type as well as our own families.

Other memories come flooding back as Noreen recalls her time in Hampshire:

Socially we used to have some great times. There were usually two, or sometimes three, dances every week and we would try not to miss those. On other occasions we went to the local pubs, of which there were many to choose from, and sometimes on a Sunday night we went to the pictures. They always seemed to show horror films, but I did manage to see some of the war films, including *In Which We Serve*. Wonderful they were, and they really raised the spirits. On the way home, sometimes there were air raids and we used to take cover in the ditches or hedges to avoid the shrapnel.

Some things were not so good, I have to say. I think the worst thing was the cold and wet. Everyone suffered from chilblains on their knees, fingers and toes. It was only in 1942 that we were issued with overcoats.

Going to work in the early morning was always full of surprises. It was nothing to open the door of the shed and find it full of sleeping soldiers who had been out on exercise all night. Sometimes the farm would come under attack when they were carrying out mock battles. We had Bofors guns on the farms and the crews lived in tin huts, so we were never short of a hot cup of tea.

The former cinema in Romsey, now a thriving theatre, was popular with WLA and service personnel alike. *(Private collection)*

The first job I had, well, I left after a few weeks because the farmer made rude suggestions, and not knowing what to do, I went home. Then I had to report to the local representative of the WLA, an elderly spinster who knew nothing of the world. She just said that I should expect farmers to be crude because they were hard-living men. Then the next job, I had to empty the lavatory bucket, so I left that as well.

Getting a bath was another thing. At my first billet we got a bath every Saturday at lunchtimes. At another farm there was no bath at all, so a local WLA official offered us the use of her bath twice a week. In another place we used to fill up a trough in the dairy and bath in that. It was cold and not very hygienic.

Later in the war Noreen was to meet a lot of service personnel.

Where I was stationed there were a lot of servicemen in billets and in camps everywhere. It was often a matter of they were here today and gone the next. I met my husband when I was nineteen – he was with the Royal Marines. But we met all nationalities, and I remember there were a lot of Australians who were shipped out to North Africa. We also saw RAF chaps who were being treated in a burns unit that was nearby. They used to travel in to the pictures on the same bus as us.

When the build-up to D-Day began, we knew something was going on because all the soldiers were confined to barracks and not allowed to speak to us. On the morning of D-Day we woke to the sound of hundreds of planes overhead, a loud, constant sound. Army lorries were being waterproofed at the farm in readiness for those men who were in one of the following waves of landings in Normandy.

One particular day, Noreen waved the soldiers off.

Well, we had to get the milking done, and then we sat on the fence and watched the convoys passing. We were waving, really high-spirited, and we shouted out 'Good luck!' to the men. It was an exciting but nevertheless strange time, really. Many of those poor chaps of course would be killed before the eventual end of the war, but for that moment in time there was so much exuberance and good feeling, almost euphoria, after the long slog of the previous years of war, and now we knew the end could well be in sight.

Within a couple of days the whole area fell eerily silent. I remember the roads were littered with cast-off equipment and so on, and for a long time after we would see farm workers and others wearing items of US uniform, and some wore Army boots.

Noreen was invited to add a final comment or two, and said:

I regret none of my time in the Women's Land Army, and I would do it all over again. Life on the land and the camaraderie of so many girls from all different backgrounds, all of us doing our bit for the war effort. It was an utterly unique and memorable experience and changed my outlook on life, and my life itself.

Keith Campbell is an Australian by birth and he served with the Royal Australian Air Force (RAAF). After one particular operation he became a prisoner of war. He gives the perspective of a member of the forces of the Commonwealth. He arrived in England via Canada:

Having spent nine months over in Canada in what was called the Empire Air Training Scheme, I was used to the same bright lights that we had at home. No blackouts, and of course an ample selection of food. When we went to England, we experienced real shortages, the blackout and wartime conditions. It was a shock to the system.

I arrived in England on the SS *Louis Pasteur* after a fast, unescorted crossing of the Atlantic. Then all the RAAF chaps were put on a train for Hampshire, where there was a holding centre for aircrew prior to posting to advanced training schools.

I flew as a bomb aimer at the operations training unit. We had Wellingtons, which were no longer front-line aircraft and which were no longer required by the operational squadrons. I also flew in Halifaxes, which were recognised to be somewhat underpowered, and they could not attain operational height with a full bomb load. They also had problems with the rudder because of a design fault. These aircraft, too, were operational rejects. Later, however, I was to experience flying in the new Mark III versions, and they were greatly improved, with a powerful radial engine.

Free time, of course, had to be enjoyed whenever it could be taken:

When not required for flying duties we aircrew had quite a lot of free time. Once we had reported to the flight office, first thing in the morning, and found that we were not required for duty, we often went into the local town, either to the pub or a dance or just visiting. We had one operational week off in every six, and then we would visit friends or relations, or we would just explore the Hampshire countryside. Many of us took advantage of the Lady Ryder Scheme, which was for aircrew on leave and allowed us to visit estates and other venues as guests.

Keith was to become a PoW after one operation:

On one operational sortie my aircraft was hit by flak and exploded when we were just outside Stuttgart. We had just set a course for home when I was suddenly blown out through the front of the aircraft. By lucky chance I had my parachute clipped on. I landed in a wheat field somewhere south-west of the city and I began to walk. I was picked up by the Germans four days later, very hungry, very tired and with no hope by then of reaching the Swiss border.

After being captured, I was taken to the interrogation centre at Oberursel, Frankfurt. I spent four days in solitary confinement, replying to questions with my name, rank and number. I was then transferred to the main compound, where I was handed a Red Cross parcel of clothing. Illegal radios in some of the camps were used to receive the information about the Normandy landings. Later, in January 1945, the Russians were advancing rapidly and our captors told us to be prepared to evacuate the camp at one hour's notice. Within three months we were liberated by the Russian Army.

Certain memories of those times are particularly poignant for Keith:

There was always some tension when an op was on, and one wondered whether it would be a long trip over Germany, or maybe just an easy one. You had to have a positive philosophy by thinking, 'It can't happen to me. I will get back.' Many of the crews followed a routine such as 'wetting' the tail wheel before getting on board the aircraft. Others made sure the mascot, such as a teddy bear, was safely in place.

On returning from a mission, of course, there was always great relief of survival, but, as happened, friends did not return, so a wake was held for them at the local pub or the mess. It stopped you becoming introverted. The odds were always stacked against you on every op. That's the way it was, and so many men had to die to bring about victory.

11

The Americans

. . . and there was flag-waving and cheers and tears.

(Dawn Gould)

The friendly invasion of Britain by soldiers, sailors and airmen from the United States is well documented. The impact of the Americans on the peoples of this island is still felt by the many who met the GIs, those who married GIs and those who became the mothers of GI war babes. Here we consider the words of a few of the ordinary men and women whose lives were affected in some small way by the Yanks.

Eileen Cheeseman, late of Highcliffe, recalled:

Then came the Americans. It was quite a culture shock for us all when they arrived. One of the most striking things, I suppose, was the aeroplanes – you know, the bombers – because almost all of them had paintings on the fuselage of scantily clad girls. There was nothing like that on the English planes, and of course, almost naked ladies were not seen in magazines, let alone on the huge aeroplanes. It was rather risqué in those days.

They were no trouble at all. We used to watch them up near the airfield and they went by sometimes, eating chicken legs. That was a real novelty, because of course we were all on rations and yet these chaps would eat more in a day than we would eat all week. Well, that's the way it seemed.

One soldier asked me if I would sew pin-tucks down the front of his uniform shirt. I think he was of Italian origin and seemed to think that all women could do that sort of thing. I did manage to finish it, although I confess my sewing skills were not that good. I thought about how his sergeant might react to his asking me to do that to his uniform, but who knows, the chap may have been the sergeant himself. I didn't know how to identify the different ranks.

Mary Shipman's husband, Bob, was an American who so loved England that he stayed here:

I met Bob and we dated before he went off on the Normandy campaign. Strangely enough, I was never frightened during that time. I never thought that anything could happen to him. No, I was never frightened.

He then went back to the States, and I would have been absolutely shattered if he hadn't come back, but it never crossed my mind that he wouldn't. It was Bob's idea, he wanted to come back.

Bob confirms this, saying:

It was a case of I wanted to come back home. I had got so used to the English ways and to her mother, who had spoilt me rotten, so that suited me just fine. I then went to Bristol University, where I got my degree as an architect, and here we are today, still married and happy.

Taken from the notes of the USAF 313th Fighter Squadron based at Winkton, near Ringwood:

Our 39 Officers and 251 men stepped onto British soil at 01.15 hours on April 15th. One man had succumbed to the voyage, Sgt. Sella being transferred to the surgeon to take care of his pneumonia. Although many written descriptions have been made of debarkation, there is still much to be said and written about the long lines of men with helmets concealing all individual features and merging them into a heterogeneous mass of fighting men slowly making their way down the gangplank. The remarks passed, the grunts and curses, the prayers of thanks for a safe passage, all blend with the sounds that go with such a movement.

By 01.30 hours the squadron was entrained, the train being on the pier. Hot coffee and doughnuts were served to everyone by the Red Cross, with much praise for the Red Cross and even more admiration for the girls serving. The train ride was an experience never to be forgotten, the compartments in the cars were littered with equipment, sleeping men, K rations.

We detrained at Lymington and were met by trucks and for the first time we heard that tents were to be our quarters. The mud on the feet of the advance party who met us at the train was a grim reminder that we were not at a picnic.

As a child, Jude James experienced the bombing of his community. He also witnessed the horror of war when, in a state of shock, he saw a car in flames, its driver motionless in the front seat. But, like a lot of children, he was amazed and fascinated by the Americans when they arrived in his part of the world.

We couldn't have done it without them, could we? They were tremendously important, vital in fact.

Their uniforms were much smarter than the British ones and they had more money, of course. It was obvious to everyone, because many of the British soldiers, particularly, used to complain about this. They wondered why the American privates and corporals and so on should have much more money than their English counterparts.

As a child, one could pick up on this tension. And of course, the Americans with their Hollywood accents and their slightly exotic sense were attractive to the girls. I had two sisters at the time and both were in the services. The Americans would call to me, 'Have you got any sisters, sonny? Bring them along.' It was a case of 'we don't want to talk to you so much as to be talking to your sisters'.

One of the girls upon whom the Americans made a lasting impression was Esther Pring.

They used to pick us up from camp and take us to wherever they were based nearby – for a dance, you know, and all the lovely food that we never had. They were very good to us, and when we were at Bovington Camp [Dorset] they came over to get all their rations and equipment and I would be loading a truck. They used to run over and say they were used to loading trucks and they would help out because they weren't busy right then. They were gentlemen. Our boys would say, 'Well, get on with it then.'

It was not all fun and laughter, and quickly forged friendships were often to last only a few days or weeks. Fleeting moments of happiness were soon to be replaced with heartbreak and anguish as American friends died in combat overseas. Dawn Gould shares her story of her brief time with a gentleman from the south.

I was a messenger in the ARP, so in my uniform and on my bike I was able to go in and out of all sorts of places where civilians would not be permitted.

There were so many of them, so many thousands of sailors and soldiers and airmen, and they all seemed so tall and healthy and handsome that nobody could help falling for them. I tell my granddaughters now, if you refused nine of them, there would still be a tenth one come along, even taller and even more handsome. We were used to having lots of handsome English sailors about, but of course they were different, the Americans. It was the accent, we liked that. It was the same as the Hollywood films – I think that did it.

He watched me when I was jitterbugging, he watched me when I got up to sing with the band. He came over to my mother and asked if he could take me out. 'She's only sixteen and has never been out on a date in her life – are you a gentleman?' And he said, 'Ma'am, I'm a southern gentleman', and mother let me go out to the pictures with him the next night. I think we queued up for about two hours, and in the end we never got to see the film so he just walked me home again. That was our first date!

I never found out where he died, or when, but I believe it was about two weeks after D-Day. Many hundreds of girls married 1st Division men and some of them come back here for the annual commemorative parade and others, like me, who lost their fiancés, still have a quiet weep every now and then.

Extract from the USAF 50th Fighter Group Daily Log:

Tuesday June 6th 1944. D-Day.
Gp. Hq. The appointed hour arrived and never had the Advance Landing Ground at Lymington presented a more beautiful or spectacular sight as one P-47 after another with navigational and dome lights winking took off from East to West, made a left-hand pattern and joined up with his fellows. In the space of minutes after the first plane was airborne the sky seemed full of circling lights in orderly sequence and much to the delight of Lt Bill Dailey, the Weather Officer the moon appeared from behind a rift of clouds and it became apparent that the sky was clearing, a good omen. As the last plane cleared the runway smoothly, every officer and enlisted man on the field wished them Godspeed and turned his thoughts to the invasion beaches and the grim work there going on.

Ann Parnaby has fond memories of the Americans, and especially their generosity in donating food to supplement the rations:

Some of the local bed and breakfast places and hotels were used as billets for the Americans. Many were billeted in Allenhurst Road, Bournemouth, near where we lived, and I remember they held parades in Warren Road.

Dad got to know some of them, especially a chap called Kellcheck, and another whose name was Julius. They used to come over to the house for tea and I know that Mr Kellcheck had got married when he was nineteen and had left his wife and a young baby at home in America. It must have been dreadful for him and the family he left behind. I suppose it was the same for all young men who had been drafted into the Army and had to serve thousands of miles away from home. That's why many families used to take care of the GIs, and other soldiers too, including the Canadians who were stationed in the area.

Well, we used to have oranges and bananas, such a treat and a wonderful way of cheering everyone up. A taste of the sun, and perhaps an indication that life was somehow going to get better. The American chef used to make delicious pastry cases about three and a half inches deep, and fill them with plum jelly

Beaches on the Hampshire coast were used by American troops for training for D-Day. (*Author's collection*)

and sultanas. When the chaps left for D-Day, I remember we were given eight tins of this lovely pudding.

They also came to the house and asked my mum how much butter we had. Butter? We didn't have enough margarine, let alone butter. They simply gave us packs and packs of butter to fill that larder. They also gave us kids lots of Oh Henry bars and packets of Lifesavers, a sort of mint fruit sweet.

The Americans were always kind, and I remember how, when they were on parade, they would pass oranges along the lines until they reached the children standing at the side of the road, and I remember once I was watching them from my bedroom window and they made every effort to throw some up to me – but their sergeant was not too impressed.

When they left the area, some of the local girls were pregnant, but that's what used to happen in war – you lived for the day and took what pleasure you could for the moment. People could be dead the next day. I think many of the girls went to America at the end of the war and some married their GIs.

The notes made by Andy Wilson of the 507th Fighter Bomber Squadron, stationed near Ringwood, record:

I was a witness to the crash of Capt Ray Langford's plane and I can still see it in my mind's eye years later. I was on the south side of the east–west runway. His plane was struggling to pull up, heading east. The nose of the plane came up. It sailed nose up without climbing. It hit something (brush?). Wing tanks of gasoline fell off and flamed. It mushed [crashed] out of sight, nose up, tail down, very scary. And out of sight – until we heard that he had survived and was discovered sitting, very shocked, with a shocked lady, in her sitting room in the first street from the airstrip in Bransgore.

First Lieutenant Robert W. 'Bob' Green had his close call on take-off also, banged a wingtip in the tops of some trees, since cut down. And Freddie Fredendall could only say, 'I heard the music, that's as close as I want to come', when he returned from a three-hour mission with his tail wheel doors peeled back like the top of a sardine can, and jammed with brush after skimming a three-foot hedge at the west side of the field on take-off.

Most anxious men of the month were First Lieutenant Duane D. 'out-Hout' Inthout, sweating out his plane the first time one of our new pilots flew it on a mission, and Capt 'Lad' Lutman hounding the S-2 section for his Air Medal. 'It's not that the Lad is really worried about the medal,' he would say. 'Hell, a little ribbon don't mean a damn to me. But if I get enough of them fast enough I might get back to see the wife and kids by Christmas, see.'

Good-natured 'Lad' also rated some sort of recognition as the most browned-off man in the squadron on the 11 May escort mission to Saarbrucken when his flight was fired upon three times by B-24s. 'Hell,' he said, 'if those guys shoot at me again I'm going to shoot back. It's them or me. We were going down to protect a straggler and they were just firing all over the place.'

Marjorie Mathew of Lymington smiles as she recalls the arrival of thousands of Americans:

The Americans were so light-hearted it seemed to take all the edge off the grimness of war. It was alive because, you see, there were all these young men in their very smart uniforms and they all seemed so cheerful. I mean, obviously they could be killed the next day. But they were always so cheerful and it was infectious. And it was weird of course, because suddenly they were all gone, and the atmosphere dropped right away when they left to go overseas. They didn't seem at all worried. I think it must have been the upbeat American personality.

The arrival of the Americans had an impact on everyone on the Home Front. *(Author's collecton)*

Poppy Butcher remembers:

> The arrival of the GIs had a great impact. The black GIs arrived first and we had never seen anything like the Americans before. When the white GIs arrived there used to be fights at the dances between them all. Yes, a great impact, and I am sure it changed our outlook.
>
> My dad had been killed in the early part of the war and there was only my mother and me, and I wasn't allowed to do certain things – if you know what I mean. We went out in crowds with the Americans, and dances of course were always a favourite.

Geoff Burrows, a schoolboy at the time, recalls:

> Yes, we all remember the Americans. Some of them went out with local school-teachers, and for us kids it was great fun as we spied on them. One teacher arrived one day on a new bike and all sorts of rumours went round as to how and where she got it.

Dawn Gould recalls:

When the Yanks left for D-Day they went from the Pavilion, and as they did so
they threw their spare coins out to the children and there was flag-waving and
tears and cheers.

❖ ❖ ❖

Notes from the log of the 313th Fighter Squadron USAF:

June 6th 1944
At 03.28 hours the squadron took off with the rest of the Group for a patrol over
Utah and Omaha beaches. The 50th Fighter Group was the first American
Group in operations against the enemy that morning. We patrolled between
8,000 and 12,000ft as cover for the beaches. No enemy aircraft were seen, and

US soldiers on their way to embarkation. *(Author's collection)*

just before leaving the pilots saw the first American troops streaming up the beaches from their landing craft.

Betty Hockey of the Non Stops concert party:

When visiting the HQ of the American Red Cross, which was in Marsham Court, one of the commandeered hotels, we had with us our soprano, Peggy, who worked there as a Welfare Officer. She told us that, if a young girl came through her door with a baby wrapped in a shawl completely covering its face, you could bet your boots that it was a black baby. Of course, in those days it was a great shame to have a baby, and even more shame to have a black baby, especially as the black troops did not have the same status as the white ones. But now, they are all treated with the same dignity.

Joyce Wilkinson of Bransgore:

I remember, before the airfield was built at Holmsley they demolished a lot of properties to make way for the runways and buildings. The area included Hill Farm, which was one of the first places to be demolished, and then houses

Joyce photographed at Holmsley. *(J. Wilkinson)*

including Vernon's, Gardener's Cottage, Whitfield's, Voss Farm and Heather Moor all went under the bulldozers. When the Americans arrived at the airfield and started raids into Europe, we used to watch the take-offs and landings of the huge aircraft. I know this sounds harsh, but when some of the aircraft returned they were badly damaged and as they landed they slid off the runway in all different directions. We used to watch them from the end of the main runway and we laughed, not really thinking that there were people inside who were injured or who might die as a result of the plane crashing. To some extent I think most people were immune to that sort of thing. You could not take everything you saw too seriously, otherwise you would go mad with the worry and upset. Our emotions were all confused – we must have laughed instead of crying because it kept us sane in a strange way.

Another member of the Non Stops concert party recalls:

When the Americans were at Stoney Cross Airfield, after one of the shows we all went mad and clambered into the Jeeps. We then raced alongside the planes as they were taking off. Yes, the US forces seemed to be a law unto themselves and did mad, mad things. This sort of behaviour was not tolerated with the British forces, who were much more strait-laced.

Elizabeth Carpenter remembers:

We had a few bombs drop around here, and later the Americans came and the whole village was swamped with soldiers. Some of the Americans were black GIs, and in those days there was a lot of stigma about that but we didn't take that much notice. I know that they had some of the worst jobs, like standing guard over the bomb dump and cleaning the vehicles. They were always friendly, but we never accepted any sweets from them. I think at that age we were a little frightened and overawed by it all.

The old coach house in Burley village is a tea room now, but it used to be a garage. The Americans had some people in there and when I was in the village one day there was a fire, and I saw this soldier running out of the building and he was on fire. He ran to the other side of the road where there was an incinerator and he threw himself into the cold ashes and rolled over and over to try and put the flames out.

Pauline Natividad lives in Southampton and is the proud daughter of a GI dad. She is a living legacy of those times and she is happy for it.

My dad was a US Army medic and he was a veteran of Omaha. I remember, as a child of about nine or ten years of age, going into a local telephone box and

The young Pilar Natividad.
(*P. Natividad*)

opening the big heavy door and getting the book down to see if this man, Paul Natividad, was in the Southampton phone book. I had been told about my dad in the early 1950s, although to me at that age, whether he was an American or not, he was my dad, and I thought I could find him locally. I thought everyone in the world was in that book.

I was searching for Paul Natividad, as my father was known to my mum, and after years of searching I discovered that Paul was his nickname – his real Christian name was Pilar. Once I had the correct name everything came to a quick conclusion. I had a hunch about three names I subsequently came across, although after phoning one of the three guys, having discounted the others, I realised I was talking to a half-brother I never knew I had, and who didn't know about me! He gave me the phone number for my dad. At almost forty years of age I traced the dad I had never known.

When I contacted him it was a big shock for him, a tearful but so happy experience for me. He had known about me and was delighted I had found him. The very next day my work colleagues at the time had a collection for my air ticket, and I was able to go to America for that Christmas. In less than a month of first speaking to my dad, I was on my way to meet him.

It was a wonderful reunion that still makes me cry, thinking about it now. I was totally accepted by him and the rest of the family and I have been going back and forth ever since. It's truly the best thing that ever happened to me. It's made me whole, it's good.

Rita Lange, also of Southampton, has a GI dad.

I bumped into a friend in the street one day and we got talking about my dad. I had known about him for some time and was keen to trace him. Anyway, the friend suggested I go to visit her aunt, who was able to give me an address in the States through which one could get information about former servicemen in England during the war.

One of the many postcards written by Pilar (Paul) to Pauline's mum. *(P. Natividad)*

I wrote off to them, and a couple of weeks later I received a reply. It said something like, we have two men on the records, one is in New York and one is in Detroit, and we think the man in Detroit is the man you are looking for. I then phoned the telephone number given and I spoke to the man. It was my dad.

I was invited on to national TV to talk about my search for my dad, and to my surprise the TV company gave me a ticket to America. When I arrived there, I spotted the man who was my father. I could tell straight away, a big tall man. The first cuddle is what I wanted. It was as though he had just been living down the street.

A wartime snapshot of Rita's father. *(R. Lange)*

Rita Lange with her
father (seated) during
the reunion.
(R. Lange)

He remembered everything – the town hall in Eastleigh where he met my
mum. He remembered my grandparents, because they used to invite him home
to tea. My father's family were the first Negroes to buy land in the area where
they lived, and it's still there. I am very proud of them all.

Edna Simmons emigrated to America with her GI husband. She still has family
living near Southampton.

Apparently he wrote to his parents and said, 'I have met the girl I am going to
marry.' It took about two years, and during that time my parents changed their
minds about the relationship. They really didn't think he was right for me. He

was older than me and they thought that was 'iffy'. Anyway, they finally gave in when I was nineteen years old and then I married him. It must have been right, because it lasted a long time and we had four beautiful children.

While there is no doubt in the minds of many of those who came into contact with the Americans that they were courteous, generous and here to help, there were occasions when the lifestyle of the American forces caused some disquiet among the population. In particular, it was difficult for the British people on rations to understand how the Americans were able to enjoy luxuries, including chocolate and fruit. It was even more difficult to understand why the British troops were unable to benefit from better rations on a par with those of the Americans.

Betty Driver recalls:

The awful thing was, if you went to our camps to sing, there was never much to eat for us or the servicemen and women. They did not have very good rations. But when we went to the American camps, the food was fantastic, and it made us angry to see our boys with rations and the Americans with 'luxury' food.

When the first American troops arrived, there were no organisations set up for them by the US authorities, and it was the Women's Voluntary Service (later the WRVS) that was called upon to welcome and feed the men at the docks. Local WVS members opened up their homes and offered hospitality as best they could. Because troop movements were surrounded by secrecy, it was impossible to give adequate notice of the arrival of men, and so the WVS had to prepare themselves for improvised welfare and hospitality arrangements.

All the WVS canteens were open to the Americans, and the sevicemen soon realised and appreciated that the women would help darn socks, change shoulder flashes on uniforms and provide information on fêtes, dances and events at which the Yanks could meet the locals. Given that some difficulties arose from what was called the private hospitality scheme, introduced to help the Americans acclimatise and to meet British people, the WVS conceived the British Welcome Club, which helped to integrate the US servicemen with local communities. In Ringwood, Hampshire, for example, forty pilots based at RAF Hurn were invited to a party to meet families in the neighbourhood and visit their homes. It was a great success, witnessed by British and American Welfare Officers, and the pilots were very loud in their appreciation of their hosts. Subsequently a list of local families who would welcome enlisted men was given to the authorities, and new friendships were forged and maintained, in some cases, long after D-Day.

Many thousands of members of the WVS participated in providing support for American hospitals in Britain and undertook simple jobs such as providing flowers, organising a library service, taking convalescents for walks and staffing kitchens during temporary emergencies.

The service given to the Americans by the WVS was far from one-sided, as is illustrated by the events at WVS hostels at Christmas. A number of Father Christmases arrived in Jeeps, trucks, and even tanks, to the delight of the little children, all of whom were given presents, sweets and attention probably beyond their expectations.

Betty Hockey again:

By 1943 the American forces were beginning to come into the country by the thousands, and the demands upon our concert party were increasing by the day. They just loved child entertainers, so my daughter Gloria and her little friend Jill, both then about four or five years old, came into their own. They often accompanied our concert party when appropriate, but mainly they were in demand for children's Christmas parties and suchlike. Their little tutus made them look very cute, and when they dressed as fairies they both helped Santa hand out presents. Of course, they were amply rewarded by the Americans, who gave both girls some wonderful presents of their own.

Few things have contributed more to the memory of the Anglo-American relationship during the Second World War than the enthusiasm with which the American airmen and soldiers entertained the children and gave away their candy and gum, to the delight of the British youngsters.

In the words of Susan Cooper, who was nine years of age and living near Tadley when the Yanks came:

Looking back, it was like having all your birthdays on one day. The Americans were always kind to the children. Many of them, of course, had their own families and must have missed them so much. They adopted us, I suppose, and treated us very well. I know some of the adults had a few moans and groans, but as a child you didn't understand them. You just enjoyed the parties, the little gifts, simple things like the carving one man made from a piece of wood and gave to me before he left. We were all skinny little kids in hand-me-down clothes, but we were happy and the Americans gave us some good times. None of us knew of course that these men faced an uncertain future. We just didn't understand.

You look back now and wonder what happened to those people who did, after all, have a great impact at a time in your life when you were very impressionable. For that moment in time, I will never forget the Americans.

12

The Children Remember

Later I saw a Lancaster bomber returning on fire and then crashing as it tried to land. That was horriible, and it had a lasting impression on me.

(John Eburne-Brown)

On the Home Front, the children were curious and innocent onlookers as their parents fought to preserve their way of life and protect them from the realities and horrors of war. Some of those children give their memories here.

In this letter from America, we hear from David Todd, who, just after the war, lived on the former RAF site at Holmsley in the New Forest, Hampshire.

Well, I was born down in Grove Road in Christchurch. It was in 1942, so midway through the war, and Christchurch was part of Hampshire then. Mum had a flat which was part of the house of my godparents, and we were there until my Father returned from wartime service. We then moved to what was called the Beech House Site. This used to be used by the RAF and our accommodation was in an old Nissen hut, which were quarters for the nearby aerodrome. If memory serves me correctly, our hut – sorry, house – was number two.

Beech House now is a modern replacement of the original very old building that was there when we were housed on the site. To the right of our house was a concrete road that led down to the main road, and at the junction was a small shop and post office.

Of course, it's not all down to my memory; some of what happened was told to me by relatives and I have researched much of my wartime history as well. Anyway, as for schooling, just down on the left of what is now a private road to East Close Hotel was the first school I ever attended. It was another wartime building, and it was just a single room. It was here that I took my first steps in reading, and I remember that my teacher was just not impressed by the fact I could pronounce the word 'that'. The building is no longer standing, although the foundations are still there. The powerhouse and the camp squash court were also in the same location and they are both still standing, so far as I know. From those humble beginnings at the one-room school, I went on to the school in the nearby village of Sopley.

I mentioned the road at the side of our house at Beech House Site; if I was well behaved, my father would give me the great treat of riding pillion on his maroon Red Enfield. We never went on the main road, of course, but I would still enjoy this treat before Dad went off to work at Escor Toys in Purewell, Christchurch.* I walked back up the track thinking I had been almost to the ends of the earth!

The woods just across the road were very much as they are today, and I used to enjoy getting lost in there and sitting for what seemed like hours, looking at the red squirrels and whatever other creatures crossed my path. Just further on, near the main road, was a large field, and more woods at the far end. I was quite scared of that area because, for some reason, I got it into my head that the wolf from *Peter and the Wolf* lived in there. Goodness knows where I got that silly idea from!

Towards the Lyndhurst end, due east of the Beech Hill Site, was the estate manager's lodge, although maybe it was for a tenant farmer. I was 'encouraged' by others to go scrumping for apples from the adjacent orchard, and once I even took my old tin wheelbarrow. Needless to say, I got caught after being chased by a chap carrying a shotgun across his forearm. I never went scrumping again. The thought of a night in the cells at Christchurch police station was more than enough to set me on the straight and narrow. Past the orchard were some houses, and my mum had a friend who lived there. They stayed in touch until a few years ago, although I am not sure what happened to the friend after all those years.

As a family we would often walk over to the main part of the aerodrome, and luckily I was allowed to go up the stairs into the control tower. It was by now derelict, even though the planes had only recently left for good. I used to imagine Spitfires taking off and landing, although at the time I didn't know whether there were Spitfires at Holmsley. I would also run up and down the runway with my arms outstretched, trying to take off. That was good fun, but I felt sorry for my new sister, who had just to sit and watch from the pram.

I was always worried that the planes coming in to land would crash into the tall weeds that were growing up through the cracks in the runway, but my mother reassured me that no planes were landing there any more.

These recollections, transcribed from original notes, are from Geoff Burrows:

---

* This company has been in business since 1914, and is now located in Bournemouth. The unique toys were originally designed by a Mr E.S. Corner, so it is not too difficult to work out how the company got its name!

In the summer of 1939 all the houses on the estate on which I lived were issued with 'Anderson' air-raid shelters. Well, at any rate, they were piles of corrugated iron sheets of various sizes and shapes delivered ready for assembly. All the local men got together into a team and the strongest chaps dug out deep holes and the rest followed on and erected the shelters in the holes. We children were kept well away in case our sensitive ears learnt some new words! Afterwards, while the men went to quench their thirst, all the women and children had to cover the shelters with the soil, until they were virtually buried.

On the day war was declared we all listened to the announcement on the radio, then we heard the siren sounding the alert. After a short while, and some confusion about what to do, the 'all clear' sounded. Two doors away lived a family, and the head of the household was a merchant seaman. His wife stood on the back doorstep, crying and hollering, 'I'll never see my man again!'

After that, Father thought that we should have a look in the shelter, to make it habitable in case we really needed it. The gardens were made up with a layer of shallow soil on top of a thick layer of heavy clay. This had been difficult enough to dig out, but underneath that was bright yellow sandstone. This had been excavated for about a foot to allow the shelters to be dropped in deep enough to meet the instructions supplied with the kits.

We children were not all that unhappy about the start of the war. A new school had been built for us and was due to open in September. However, there were no air-raid shelters there, and the authorities would not open the school until they were built. So we had an extended holiday, until the end of October in fact, before we started back to our lessons.

One irksome requirement was having to carry a gas mask with you at all times. A policeman or warden could have you arrested if you didn't have it with you. They were issued in a little cardboard box, but Mother bought imitation leather cases with a shoulder strap for ours.

There were also little wooden platforms about a foot square, mounted on posts about three feet high, with special green paint on them. Apparently, if there had ever been a gas attack the paint would have changed colour. Most of them were near to Wardens' Posts, and the Air Raid Wardens carried football rattles and, I believe, whistles that would have been used as a warning to put on our masks.

The first signs of war were a few low flights made by overenthusiastic Spitfire pilots, but that was a very brief event. Then came the installation of anti-aircraft guns on one or two open spaces locally, and my, what a noise they made! They made the ground shake. There were also a number of searchlights, mounted on the backs of large Army lorries.

More spectacular, I suppose, were the barrage balloons that were situated all over the town. When they were moored close to the ground they looked huge, but they were normally a hundred feet or so aloft, ready to be put up high in case of an air raid. We always knew when a raid was imminent, because they went up to a great height. Hence, I believe, the expression 'when the balloon goes up'. The base sites usually had a huddle of tents and lorries, and little else.

Recreation is a good tonic in wartime! Crew enjoying a few moments of play at a barrage-balloon site of the type seen in some parts of Hampshire. *(Author's collection)*

The balloons could be seen clearly on moonlit nights, and as far as I know not one was hit by a German bomber. However, I did twice see them brought down by lightning – the second time I actually saw the lightning strike. They came down in a mass of flames, and Father said that the ground crews were in grave danger of being injured by the heavy steel cable as it crashed down.

There were lots of railway bridges in the town, and large concrete blocks were cast on the roads underneath. Traffic had to zigzag between them. Next to the blocks on the road were piles of steel girders and old tram lines. The idea was that, if the Germans landed, the steel would be wedged between the concrete blocks so that the road would be impassable.

Air raids started in earnest later in 1940 and it got so bad that we didn't wait for the siren, we just went straight to bed in the shelter. It was quite cosy, with bunk beds and a little box on which stood a Tilley lamp, which we used to boil a kettle for tea when the Ack-Ack was too loud to let us sleep. Sometimes the 'all clear' was given around midnight or one o'clock, and we would go back into the house and to bed.

The town centre was badly bombed, and the down-town schools were used as emergency accommodation. This meant those children had no school to go to, so schools like ours on the outskirts went part time. We did one week eight o'clock until noon, and the alternate week one o'clock until five o'clock. The town children were brought by buses, and they did the other half of the day and shared our desks. Towns used to help each other out with loaned transport when their own fleet of buses, for example, had been damaged or had been blown to bits.

There were very few daylight air raids, but we did occasionally see the insides of the shelters at school. If we were in more than half an hour, we were issued with chewing gum. If it was more than an hour, we were given a drink of (very stale, flat) water.

The town centre was a mess, and it took ages to clear up the rubble, though the main roads were cleared fairly quickly. Large cast-iron pipes were laid along the side of many roads to replace damaged water mains. They were an additional hazard when walking in the blackout. They were partially buried where they crossed roads. Trolleybuses had to be pushed or towed where the wires were down, though the overhead crews were very quick to repair damaged sections.

The most frightening things to be dropped on us were the parachute mines. They had any amount of explosives between 2½ and 5 tons, and you could see them slowly floating down in the moonlight, gradually getting closer. There was nothing you could do except shelter, but one fell nearby and wiped out not only a whole street but the air-raid shelters as well. One night I found an incendiary bomb that had failed to go off. I kept it in my toy box until Father came home from the Army. He nearly had a fit when he saw it, and got rid of it very quickly.

I was now at grammar school, where things went on more or less as normal, though there were lots of shortages, in particular paper. We had to cut normal pages up into eighths, and learn to write very small! Both sides of the paper, of course. Most of the male teachers were either conscripted or volunteered for the armed forces, and consequently there was a preponderance of women teachers. Indeed, some of them had taught us at junior school!

In our spare time we all got involved in patriotic activities, such as growing extra food, keeping rabbits (to eat), picking rose hips and collecting waste paper. I also went to St John Ambulance classes and learnt some basic first aid. We children were often used as patients for the adults to practise on. On more than one occasion I had to tell the first-aider what he (or she) was doing wrong! Then we would be put on stretchers and taken for a ride in the ambulance. My, but were those wartime ambulances basic!

Air raids became fewer, but there was the occasional nuisance raid. One morning while we were still in bed, a Messerschmitt ME109 machine-gunned our street – very frightening. It was about this time that we used to find strips of aluminium foil in the streets and gardens. We learnt later that it was called window and was used to confuse the radar operators. Talking of which, we had two WAAFs billeted with us for about a year. They were at a radar station on the coast, but it was secret then, and they said they worked in radio.

There was a large wooden mock village built on the open hills nearby. Situated well away from habitation, it was set on fire to act as a decoy for the German bombers. Then it was rebuilt for the next time. I don't know whether it worked.

On another early morning, we were awakened by all the neighbours shouting. We looked out of my bedroom window, and what a sight we saw! The sea was about half a mile away, and you could see the tops of the cliffs from my window. The cause of all the commotion was a lone Heinkel bomber flying slowly on a parallel course to the cliffs, very low and with smoke pouring out of one wing. Now we knew something that the German pilot didn't: he was quickly approaching an anti-aircraft battery situated on the cliff top. We all held our breath to see what happened. There was just one bang from the gun as the plane drew opposite the battery, and the Heinkel exploded in a cloud of smoke and just disappeared. Of course, we all cheered like mad.

In 1944, limited street lighting was allowed again, called 'starlights'. They were very small, and only allowed on main roads, but were better than nothing.

One morning at school in 1944, one of the prefects came into the classroom during a lesson – that sort of thing was unheard of in those days. He spoke to the teacher, and at the end of the lesson the teacher told us that instead of going to our next lesson we were to assemble in the main hall. There the headmaster told us that it had been officially announced that the second front was open, that troops had landed on the beaches in France, and therefore it was D-Day. 'Now back to your lessons, boys.'

Rosalie Hill of Havant remembers:

I was born in 1940, so I was too young to be scared by what was happening. We were living in my nan's house and there were three families on four floors. One incident was when I asked my mum if I could get my dolly from the bedroom, which was just one floor up. I got the doll, and just a few minutes later a bomb dropped on the local library. It put the windows out in the house, including the window in my bedroom. Luckily I was not in there at the time. Anyway, Mum later took me over to see the flattened library. My husband's cousin was killed in that, but at the time I didn't know him or my husband, of course.

I also remember 'malt on sticks' and cod-liver oil on spoons with the child's name written on plaster and stuck to the spoon. Later, when we met Canadian troops, they were very kind to us and gave us drinking chocolate and lovely red apples.

John Eburne-Brown was born on 11 February 1933 to mother Vera and father Clifford. A sister, Margaret, was born several years later.

A 'polyphoto' of Rosalie aged about three. *(R. Hill)*

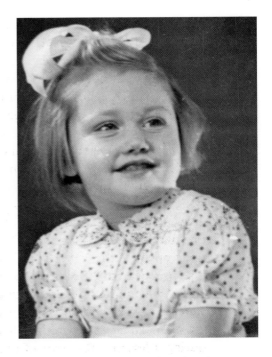

My dad was a piano tuner and an accomplished musician, and later he taught music. Mum spent all her time looking after us and the home, very much what the women did in those days. Dad had been in the First World War, and at forty years of age was not in the initial call-up programme for service in the war. He did, however, serve in the Auxiliary Fire Service.

As a family we travelled quite a lot because of the work Dad did and the opportunities for him. Dad had become a youth worker and he also managed Reception Centres for the civilian population and evacuees, and so on.

I was aged six years at the outbreak of war and I remember that a chap by the name of Squadron Leader Roland was billeted for a short while with our family. I have no idea where he was based or why he left us, but I guess the service people were always on the move, because of the demands of the war.

I do recall the arrival of evacuees locally, and I think they were actually groups who were in transit for other destinations because they were billeted only for a short while. I think they came from one of the big cities, and, compared to us, they had nothing, so my mum gave them my football to keep, which was a small token of kindness towards those children.

Later in the war a German bomber that had obviously been shot down was put on display in the car park of the Gaumont cinema, and for us children it was wonderful to be able to play in it. Another thing I remember, which at the time we all thought was a snub to Hitler and his bombers, was when we were watching the Christmas pantomime. An air-raid alert was sounded but the audience decided to stay and watch the show through the raid. We did, and we were all all right!

After the major bombing we didn't go into town for several days, but then we saw the devastation. The city centre was flattened. I think that as children we all viewed this with a mix of excitement and curiosity. We got used to classmates missing after air raids. In contrast, I remember seeing a German bomber being chased by a Spitfire. All the class cheered as the plane crashed, and we saw parachutes come from the burning plane.

One early morning I saw aeroplanes taking off from nearby airfield. Later I saw a Lancaster bomber returning on fire and then crashing as it tried to land. That was horrible, and it had a lasting impression on me.

Some major centres of population were hit hard by bombing. *(Private collection)*

Something else I remember was the garage just up our road, which we knew was involved in making munitions. There were six women employed there. Occasionally we saw barrage balloons on fire. I know that waste oil was set alight on the ground in smoke pots, and this sent palls of smoke into the sky to try and confuse the enemy bombers and obscure their view of the target area. There were rocket batteries in the local park, and they were still there after the war.

One incident I do recall with amusement is when all the vehicles were assembled and waiting to move off for the D-Day campaign. One of the older boys I knew somehow managed to start up one of the Bren-gun carriers. I don't know whether it was guarded, but he managed to get into the vehicle and then he drove in it until he was stopped by a policeman. He must have got a severe ticking-off, if not worse than that. I never found out what happened.

Chris Lewis met German PoWs:

The earliest memory is that two German prisoners of war lived in the adjoining cottage. An elder sister told me that one of them had been a pilot, or at least a member of an aircrew that had been shot down. They had obviously been through a period of imprisonment and assessment before being considered safe and able to be released to work without close supervision, on the same farm as my father. The Germans were not allowed to roam freely or to go into the nearest town, so my family did their shopping for them. One of them we knew as William (Wilhelm); he was regarded as an anti-Nazi and apparently he was quite happy to be where he was for the duration of the war. However, the other one, known as Henry (Heinz), was considered a pro-Nazi. William married an English girl after the war and remained in this country, but I do not know what happened to Henry. I spent quite a lot of time in their company and I can remember only good things. The Germans did appreciate the help given to them by my family and they repaid it by making a ship-in-a-bottle for each of my four elder sisters and my mother. Their only requirement was a square-shaped Johnny Walker whisky bottle, which I would imagine were very difficult to obtain. However, I know that they were obtained, because I still have the one that was made for my mother.

Brenda Graddidge (née Lucas) was six years and four months old when war was declared, and she remembers the first air-raid warning very well.

Prisoners of war: a common sight in many Hampshire towns, especially towards the end of the war. (*Author's collection*)

It was on the Sunday morning. We lived in a three-bedroom terrace house, that's Mum, Dad and my four siblings. We had a pantry under the stairs that was used for storing the brushes, dusters and Mum's sewing-box. Dad had cleared it out and I can remember my sister – she was five years older than me – was already sitting in there. Mum was standing by the door and Dad was sitting very near with me on his lap, ready to dive into the pantry.

Soon after this we were supplied with an Anderson shelter, which came in parts and which Dad erected in the garden. When it was in position and covered in earth, Dad made some benches, and then some steps so we could get in and out easily enough. He also made a bunk bed for me and my sister to sleep in. The condensation ran down the walls, I remember, and it smelt: it wasn't nice at all. We sat in there all huddled up, and with torches and a flask of tea. Because Dad had served in the First World War, he was too old for the Second. But anyway, he was in the Home Guard and did a lot of training. He was also an ARP Warden and a First Aid Officer, so he did his bit for the war effort.

At night we used Dad's thick Home Guard coat to cover our bed because we had very little coal and the rooms were always cold at night. I remember we had a home-made type of wheelbarrow, and we used this to collect coke, after queuing for ages. We also used potato peelings and slack to help boost the fire.

Clothes were rationed and we had to have coupons. One time my auntie acquired a bag of some type; I think it was a flour sack. Anyway, my mum unpicked it and washed it, and my sister was able to make it into a skirt and waistcoat for me. Like many other folk we used parachute silk, when some became available, shall we say, for making underwear.

My sister, whose husband was in the forces, lived in quite a large house with her baby. Because of that she had to take in people and the house was used as a billet. She was not very happy about that, because she said the people she had staying were not respectful or very nice. My sister went to work in a munitions factory while my mum looked after the little one.

My sister used to visit a local hospital to talk to the wounded soldiers. Some would come over to our house as walking wounded and others in wheelchairs. One chap from the Parachute Regiment had lost one leg and one arm and had one eye missing. How terrible!

Someone we knew who lived down our road and became a prisoner of war couldn't face life on his return and, sadly, he took his own life.

John Clifford comments:

Oddly, I have no recollection of the big air raid in May 1943 when so many buildings in central Bournemouth were destroyed, but I know that my father's Home Guard unit had to help sort things out. What I do recall, however, is the German bombers going over, night after night, en route presumably to the Midlands, and once, while at the Iford Lane trolleybus terminus, my brother and I saw some objects falling away from a plane over towards Boscombe, or

The trolleybus, a familiar sight on the streets of Bournemouth. The town formerly came within the borders of Hampshire. *(Author's collection)*

somewhere that way, German bombs, the only ones we ever actually saw. Another time, we were walking along the Overcliff Drive one evening when some German planes came over very low indeed, so low that we could see the pilots looking down, but no bombs fell on that occasion, thankfully.

John Thornley remembers:

As soon as the wailing howl of the siren started we were pulled from our beds and dragged, half asleep, down the stairs and across the garden to the air-raid shelter. There a small posse of women and children huddled anxiously together, sometimes for hours. The adults comforted themselves with cups of tea and cigarettes and talking in hushed voices, while the children tried to get some sleep.

Joan Coup's brother did not fare well during evacuation.

My brother was not so fortunate as I, when, at a much later date, he was evacuated to a farm and he was not at all happy. He was expected to do small jobs around the farm, even though he was just six years old. He never received any of his sweet ration – that must have gone to the host family – and he never received any pocket money for the jobs he did. Despite the fact there were hens

'Doing his bit'. John Thornley Snr (back row, fourth from the left) with colleagues from his RAFVR unit. (*J. Thornley*)

on the farm he was always given dried egg, as was Mother on one visit. After a few months he was taken out of that family and Mother took him back home.

Chris Lewis again:

I often visited the gun site and became a sort of mascot to the soldiers. One day, near the end of summer, the cook told me to go around the hedges and collect as many blackberries as I could. This I did, and the cook baked a blackberry and apple pie for me and my family. He used apples from the nearby orchard and Army rations for the pastry. You can imagine how welcome this was at that time! I don't know whether there is any connection, but blackberry and apple pie is still a favourite of mine.

Can you imagine what it must have been like, having large guns firing through the night as close as twenty yards or so from your house?

13

With Fondness and Regret

Great friends, hard but happy times, and the knowledge that you helped to keep the world free for future generations.

(Keith Campbell)

The six long years had brought about death and destruction, joy and sorrow, hopes and heartache, and a welding together of the nation the like of which would never be seen again. The war had changed attitudes, people and society, the world of finance, business and technology. The entire structure of everything had changed.

Elsa Hastings comments:

I look back on those wartime days with fond memories and I miss all the happy times. You try never to remember the darker days and events.

Geoff Burrows remembers:

And so we all followed the progress of the war. I had a large map on my bedroom wall, covered with coloured flags on pins. And, after what seemed an awfully long time, we knew the end was near when we heard John Snagge announce on the wireless: 'Hitler is dead, I repeat, Hitler is dead.'

Everybody began to make preparations for a party, and on VE Day a line of trestle tables was set up on the recreation ground behind our houses. I can't remember what there was to eat or drink, but with rationing it wouldn't have been much. I do remember the huge bonfire and the heat on my face, and all the lights were on in every house, with the curtains deliberately left open.

Father came home soon after that, and we went on a holiday to a cottage up in the Tyne valley. While we were there, VJ Day was announced. We were out in open country, and it seemed that every hilltop for miles around had on it a huge bonfire. The cottage had a large garden, so we had one of our own as well.

And that was the end of my war. The peace that followed was drab and miserable, without the danger and excitement of the guns and bombs. But things began to look up, and we realised that it had all been worth it.

A VE Day party – time to smile again. *(Sharon Cross, SHM)*

John Eburne-Brown served in the RAF after the war.

I served in the Royal Air Force in post-war years and it was during that time I met members of what was called the German Service Organisation. These were chaps who were helping to rebuild Germany. They were ex-soldiers for the most part, and they were quite distinguishable in their green uniforms. I enjoyed my twelve years of service, and, by talking to men who had served in the RAF during the war, I learnt much about how they coped. We owe them so much.

Keith Campbell from Australia:

Nowadays it is important to me that the comradeship of those years carries on for as long as there are enough survivors around. We used to see each other all the time, but now it's once a year at the annual reunion. In those days we relied on each other absolutely, and it's just so sad that with the passing of time our comrades are passing away. Great friends, hard but happy times, and the knowledge that you helped to keep the world free for future generations.

David Todd from the United States notes:

I was still fascinated by that airfield, and the others that were all around. I was, shall we say, rather cross when they placed holiday caravans there at Holmsley. I felt that it was rather humiliating to the men and women who had served this country so well during the war.

A member of the Women's Land Army wrote of her time in service:

> I am glad that I was living then,
> I don't regret a day,
> And that I met those boys and girls
> Who passed along that way.
> I like to think that special bond
> Made when we were young and strong
> Still lingers down the passing years,
> Like the echo of a song.

Chris Lewis kept a diary:

We still lived in the country, but things would never be quite the same again. Strangely, our accommodation was now a converted Nissen hut. We were on what was called 'E' site of a former RAF camp, and this was down a narrow road with a number of sites branching off it. Our site was at least a half a mile from the main road. The local council had taken over the camp to provide much-needed homes for local families. The accommodation had been divided up into a number of rooms, not much taller than head height, with thin walls. We now had electricity, but heating and cooking were still by a coal-fired range and one of the large stoves normally associated with barrack rooms. In the winter, the whole interior got very cold, and I can remember making ice-lollies in a glass standing on the inside of my bedroom window. The water for drinking, cooking and washing was from an outside communal tap that froze often during a hard winter, and our toilet was still outside. This wasn't the flushing type, but at least a contractor emptied the bucket regularly.

From New Zealand, Doris Paice recalls:

In later years I went back to RAF Calshot while on a visit to England and I saw some of the surviving Sunderland Flying Boats in mothballs, and the quarters were occupied by people who had been evacuated from the island of Tristan da Cunha after the natural disaster there.

Betty Hockey says:

My telephone never seems to stop ringing because I have helped a number of former GIs with various wartime research projects and they get answers, so my number gets passed on. Most requests for help are interesting, especially when it comes to finding people. I know there have been many happy reunions, but sadly not all fathers are alive, so there is often no closure for the family.

Geoff Burrows again:

During the war – it was one of those occasions that the 'alert' siren sounded again, and we got up out of bed and ran to the shelter. I always wore Dad's tin hat when this happened. As I was going into the shelter I felt a bang on the head, and I later found a groove in the steel helmet that I had been wearing.

After the end of the war, when we were removing all the soil, ready to take out the shelter, we found a 6-inch-long spear-shaped piece of shrapnel next to the entrance to the shelter. That's what made the groove in my tin hat!

An unnamed observer wrote:

One girl's mother made herself a pair of pants out of a Union Jack, and she was dancing in the street with her skirt up, proudly displaying her handiwork. A rather graphic image to close an era!

Carol Terry recalls:

Many of the dads down our road and in the local streets came home all within a few weeks of each other. Some were RAF, some Army, and a chap who had been in the Navy, I remember.

My friend Peggy waited with us all until one morning a large car came up the street and stopped outside her house. Two men went inside and she thought one might be her dad. She ran back to the house, and a little while later she came out with her mum. They came across to call on my mum.

When I got downstairs Peggy and her mum and my mum were all in tears. Peggy's dad was not coming home. He had died from a suspected heart attack on the train bringing him back. What a terrible tragedy, that he survived the war and died within two hours of getting home and being reunited with his family. Peggy's mum died three years later, they say from a broken heart. Peggy was an orphan at just ten years old. They were all victims of the war.

John Thornley Snr, a member of the RAFVR. *(J. Thornley)*

John Thornley reflects:

Looking back on my early life in those dark days, there were compensations as well as hardships. The continual need to make do and mend and

Young friends: time to celebrate at last. *(D. Bowers)*

the constant threat of death or destruction from German bombs were facts of life. We learnt not to complain and to be content with simple pleasures. Undoubtedly we were fitter and thriftier because we had no chance to indulge ourselves.

We were proud of our country and its great leader, and above all thanks to good fortune and the sacrifice of others we survived. My memories of my wartime childhood are tinged with great fondness rather than any regret.

And Doreen Bowers writes:

There was great excitement now that the war in Europe was over. Celebration parties were planned and a feeling of euphoria prevailed. It is hard to explain just how I felt, but it was an immense feeling of relief to sleep at night knowing that there would be no air raids or sounds of gunfire or bombs exploding to wake me up.

Our road was decorated with bunting, and a clown was hired to entertain the children. We had our photograph taken, and in the evening I joined my friends in visiting other street parties. We were all so very happy. Not everyone wanted to join the celebrations, because unfortunately there were those who had lost loved ones and they had no cause to be happy.

On VE Day I stood in the crowd outside Buckingham Palace, and with everybody else I shouted for the King and Queen and Winston Churchill. Over and over again they came out onto the balcony. Later we walked to see No. 10 Downing Street, and a policeman took us up to see the building. As we returned to the end of the street, Winston Churchill drove past and he smiled and gave us the victory salute. What a marvellous day it was!

As the days went by the soldiers began to return home, some of them having been away for many years. There were many happy reunions, and I watched friends running to meet fathers they hadn't seen for a long time. It was a miracle for me that none of my family had been killed or wounded in the war.

Doris Hancock says:

I remember that for most of the time throughout the war I had hand-me-down clothes from my older sister, and as they became threadbare they were replaced with gifts of clothing from some of the clothing exchanges.

When the war was nearly over, my mum asked me to make myself up really nice because Dad was coming home from the Army.

Of course all I had were second-hand clothes on my rather lean frame, and I looked like most other kids on the street. I am not sure how I could have managed to look nice in this state. However, at ten years old and with a little imagination, I decided to sew some coloured patches of cloth onto my dress to make it more cheerful. It took me hours, but by the time I was told Dad was on his way down the street, I had finished and was very proud of my handiwork.

Dad had another soldier with him, who was holding him by one arm. We shouted out and ran to Dad. He said, 'Hello girls, how nice to see you both today.' I was so happy, thinking Dad appreciated my handiwork.

Mum, who was close behind us, took Dad and us girls in her care and thanked the other man. I realised that something was not quite right. When we got into the house, Mum told us Dad was blind in one eye and had very poor sight in the other. He couldn't really see my pretty dress, but it didn't matter – he was home from the war.

Joan Coup thinks of the host family who took her in when she was an evacuee:

The time eventually came for my return home, and not unnaturally there were tears and hugs between Auntie and Uncle and

Doreen and Jean at the end of the war.
(D. Bowers)

myself, with promises to keep in touch. Even some of my school friends came to see me off.

This was not, of course, goodbye to my lovely Aunt Flo and Uncle Sam, because we kept in touch for forty years, and after I was married and had a family of my own they took them to their hearts as they had me all those years ago. Every year we spent at least part of our holiday with them.

Now, with the passing of so many years, they are, sadly, no longer with us, and I can only say a big thank you to the two strangers who were responsible for making my war a happy one. They are still alive in my heart.

Noreen Cooper, from Australia, remembers well:

After VJ Day the Women's Land Army had a parade in Southampton, through the city and ending up at the Civic Centre. We marched out of step, as you can imagine, and I remember a naval officer coming out of the crowd running alongside us shouting 'left, right, left, right'. At the Civic Centre we received our 'service' badges. Mine was for six years' service.

Actually, after VE Day I could have got my discharge because of my length of service, but to be honest, what was I going to do? There was no way I wanted to go back to working 'inside' again, so I just stayed on.

In March 1946, seven hundred of us went to Caxton Hall in London, to a rally where we asked for equal pay for equal work. Needless to say, we never got it. The men earned more than us and that's the way it was. I was married by then, and in September 1946 I left the service when I discovered I was pregnant.

Hal Ryder was just nineteen years of age when, as a sergeant in the Army, he embarked from the shores of southern England eventually to lead the men under his command onto the Normandy beaches:

I was a member of the Amphibious Combat Engineers, part of the 1st Engineer Special Brigade that was formed for the Normandy campaign. We had a total strength of 27,000 men who had the job of leading the infantry on to the beaches, and we had to remove the mines and booby traps to make the way clear for the troops.

I was nineteen then and had seventy men under my command. Within a few seconds of hitting the beach, I became ninety-one. It was a dramatic and terrifying experience, not least because of the many men under my command who died.

When people talk about D-Day they never seem to mention the noise that went with the invasion. That was really very terrifying, and you have to realise that we had two battleships firing over our heads, there were rocket ships simultaneously firing, and there were cruisers and destroyers also firing round after round over our heads at the enemy positions in front of us.

Four servicemen, representing the Allied Nations, pose for a photograph in Trafalgar Square at the end of the war. Great happiness mingled with sadness as these men would soon be saying farewell to their buddies and the comradeship that helped them through the war years. *(OP)*

I joined the Army as a Private and retired at the end of the war as a Lieutenant Colonel. After the experience of war I decided that I should do something towards bringing people together in friendship instead of conflict. So far I have taken veterans of fifty-one of the sixty-six US 1st Infantry Divisions back to England and Europe. Under the banner of Operation Friendly Invasion we have been able to bring people together from the different countries, some former enemies and some of course still our Allies, in the true spirit of unity. That's the legacy I want to leave.

The final words are those of Charles Graves:

Ignorance, jealousy and suspicion are essential factors in the tradition of re-current war. But everything that makes for mutual understanding and help, gladly given and proudly accepted between free countries, is a foundation stone, however small, for the newer and, one hopes, more sympathetic civilisation of the future.